Heart Is Where the Home Is

Peggy —
I hope you enjoy
the book — It was
written with love and
great memories.
I know we share many
great memories together
I hope there will be
many more.
Fondly,
Ruth

To order additional copies, please contact us.
BookSurge, LLC
www.booksurge.com
1-866-308-6235
orders@booksurge.com

RUTHI
MURPHY

HEART IS WHERE
THE HOME IS

2006

Heart Is Where the Home Is

TABLE OF CONTENTS

ACKNOWLEDGEMENTS

To my dear friend Gwen;
How many times did you read and edit the following pages?
It was through your persistence and drive that this book was accomplished.

To my forever friend Joan;
You read each story before anyone and then encouraged me to write more;
Thanks, for giving me the in-sight to believing in myself.

To Bill,
Who helped open my heart from the past.
How I respect your devotion to the children who presently reside in my home.

To my love and life flow;
My husband Bob, and my children,
Dan, Kathleen, Shelly and my sons-in-law Rick and Doug.
How could life ever hold such meaning without you?
Thank you for your support and genuine love.

To my beautiful grandchildren;
Zachary, Chelsea Kaiah, and Joe
You now hold my dreams for future memories.
You are surely my proof that "life carries on!"

Lastly, a special recognition is extended to my two brothers:
Jerry and Bobby
How I love you both.
No matter what circumstances placed us in the orphan home
we always had each other to rely on.
Together, we beat the odds.

FOREWORD

Sometime ago, back in the 1950's and early 60's a young girl, with blonde curly hair and soft blue questioning eyes, lived in an orphanage. She felt alone in the world even though she had two brothers that lived in the home with her. She learned through an ardent imagination, at a very early age, that she could make life interesting.

This young girl loved to read and create poetry about everything around her. She tried hard to keep her emotions in check but often had to resort to pen, paper and a quiet room. There, sitting alone with her thoughts, she could pour her emotions on paper and no one would see how she really felt about her surroundings.

This young girl was me, Ruthi Phillips Murphy. Once again, my emotions have spilled out into the words of this book. My emotions and imagination seemed to run away with me at times. However, my memories, some good and some not so good, helped to keep me focused on my endeavor.

Sitting down to write is harder than anyone can imagine but it is also more rewarding than anything I can think of. Sometimes I would find myself sitting at my desk in tears and other times in a complete fit of laughter as memories consumed the moment.

My life, through the hands of time, has taken on many roles. I find that finally, while starting another phase of life, I can say I'm proud of who I am and what I have accomplished.

I hope you enjoy this book written from the heart. I cherish it with a lot of love. Please skim through the stories and find the one that best relates to you. I'm sure there will be little sections here and there where you will find yourself, staring off into space, remembering another simpler time of your own childhood.

It means a lot to me—sharing this book of memories with you. I hope you enjoy the stories and feel the simplicity of love, hard work and dedication shown by all the people involved in this very special place— St. Vincent's, where I grew up and the place I still call home.

HISTORY OF A VERY SPECIAL PLACE

It was a cold winter in the year 1818 when the newly consecrated bishop from Louisiana, Louis William Valentine DuBourg, took residency in St. Louis. Through hard work and a strong eye for reconstruction he established a beautiful landmark known as The Old Cathedral. What a great accomplishment for this young Bishop! Little did he know that this was just the beginning of his long line of architectural achievements. His name spread far and wide as a man who could be challenged to get any job completed.

As Bishop Dubourg became familiar with this great city, his expectations for great things began to develop. There was just one obstacle that nagged at the Bishop, no matter how hard he tried to focus on the project at hand.

The number of orphaned children roaming the streets begging for food and shelter became the bishop's nightly vision. His mind would reel as he found his eyes staring into the large sorrowful eyes of these tiny souls. It became apparent that since the care of orphaned children was minimal during these early years—it would soon become the bishop's foremost responsibility. He became instrumental in obtaining several buildings to temporarily house the boys and girls that were left alone in this world needing desperately the guidance and care of benefactors. The Bishop vowed that the children would always take priority to any other of his plights.

The year 1849 was a memorable year in the history of St. Louis. There were two devastating calamities that nearly destroyed the city. A fire that had started on a steamboat at the levee edge, ravaged 23 boats and then spread quickly throughout the city burning 430 buildings within a 15 block area. This left many people out of work and homeless. Meanwhile, the city was in the midst of a cholera epidemic which left many children alone to fend for themselves. The death toll rose in the hundreds; together, the calamities claimed a total of five thousand lives.

Unspeakable misery and want were caused by these terrible disasters among a population in the city of 60,000 people. Half of that population was German immigrants who came to this great city with high hopes that soon fell prey to sickness and death. Most of the immigrants were poor and housing was very limited. Friends and neighbors did what they could to help the needy and the homeless children but that was not enough; however, there seemed to be a special definition of this tough pioneer age. Two of the greatest of virtues—generosity and strong faith triumphed.

In the year 1850 an appeal was issued to all Catholic priests and laymen to come to the aid of the German orphans who were left behind in the wake of the terrible fire and cholera disasters.

The appeal found an immediate response and the first plot of ground on Hogan Street between Cass Avenue and O'Fallon Street was bought and the first German Orphan Home was erected. Five Sisters, of the St. Joseph order, did their best to offer maternal support, taking charge of 30 orphaned children who were left alone in the city with only memories of their mothers, fathers, and family.

The first year proved to be one of great difficulty but through generous donations from benefactors, the home was up and running with six rooms, a bakery and laundry facilities.

The Sisters of Christian Charity were driven out of Germany in the spring of 1873 by the so called "Kulturkompf," which greatly curtailed Catholic teaching in that country. Work and education by the sisters came to a complete halt, leaving a lack of religion and education in their place. The sisters came to America and shortly accepted their duties as the new order of sisters to the children in the orphanage. At this time there were 19 sisters to take care of a fast growing number of orphans, now totaling 221.

Influenza broke out in the city and also in the orphanage in March of 1919. Over 100 children in the home were afflicted. Two sisters and four children died from this horrendous disease and again the home grew with more orphans left behind by yet another catastrophe.

It wasn't long until the children outgrew the home. An appeal was put forth to all the Catholic churches and organizations in St. Louis and the surrounding areas. It didn't take long before 20 acres of ground was purchased for the purpose of building a new and up-to-date home for the orphans. After careful planning and consideration, the new home was built in Normandy and the cornerstone was laid June 15, 1916. The building made rapid progress and on July 31st of the following year the first moving van appeared before the Home. By August 8th, the children were moved into their new home. The old home on Hogan Street was sold to Father Timothy Dempsey in 1920 in the pre-Depression era.

A grotto was built in 1924 as a memorial to the order of Sisters of Christian Charity. This celebrated the 50th anniversary of their arrival in the United States. Over their past 50 years the home had opened its heart to over two thousand children. The children had the comforts of home while the sisters prepared them to become useful members of society. These dear sisters stood in place of the lost mothers and fathers to the many children that were housed in the protection of the home.

The year 1941 brought two occasions of great sadness to the home. The passing away of two former students from the old home. The two lost their lives during the infamous attack on Pearl Harbor on December 7th. Another alumnus was in the Navy's Air Force and was killed in a plane crash. Four more alumni were killed during active duty while serving God and their country during the war in 1945.

The Civil War, the Great Depression, and World Wars I and II all were instrumental in bringing their share of orphans to the St. Vincent's doors.

In 1959 the orphanage underwent a major remodeling project. New lighting and living arrangements changed from a congregate system of dormitories to a new "group system" that included apartments. And in the year of 1961 as many as nine children from Cuba were offered a home at St. Vincent's. In housing these children, St. Vincent's had openly chosen to play a small part in the struggle between Catholicism and Communism.

Early in 1987 St. Vincent's Home was faced with the realization that the population of the home was changing. In the 137 years of the Home's history the children's needs were no longer that of just a lonely orphan. Now, the sisters faced a more damaged, more alienated and consequently, more needy child.

The residing children were exhibiting greater emotional problems than ever before. This change was in comparison to the orphan of yesterday, that had been conceived in love and who could remember happier days with their family. Or the child of a broken home who still held onto the love of one or both parents. St. Vincent has now become one of those special facilities we call a residential treatment center where the children have special needs twenty-four hours a day. Also, the facility is no longer called St. Vincent's Orphanage. Today it is called St. Vincent's Home.

The children came in the past, as they do today, with a sense of bewilderment and anxiety. Their lives have been turned completely upside down due to no fault of their own. It has taken many years of sacrifice, dedication and love from the sisters, the community and many benefactors here in St. Louis, to make this Home a thriving and trusted place, a place which harbors the souls of so many needy and dependent children.

The patrons who have supported the home all these years have neither expected nor desire praise. Yet, they bring their gifts and perform their works from the sole motivation of God's love and the love of His children.

Previously, the sisters not only took on the role of mother and father but of teachers, social workers, art and recreation therapists. The sisters always loved and prayed for the children. Now, in this new generation, the home runs with a highly efficient staff of lay-people who are trained and qualified to meet the children's overwhelming social, emotional, and educational needs.

They too, just as the sisters, approach each day with love and respect for the children in their care. It is, however, the love of children that has first created the foundation which makes up the heritage of this grand orphanage called "home" to many a spirited soul.

I happen to be one of the spirited souls that for 14 years was raised and loved by the Sisters of Christian Charity. Everything I am or have become is due to the tireless efforts of the dear sisters who guided and taught with gentle care. I don't know what I would have become if the courts hadn't placed me at the doors of the orphanage at the tender age of one. I am a product of the orphan home's careful intervention. I'll never be able to completely express the abundance of gratitude and love I hold in my heart for all who help make the home possible, but especially the dear sisters who dedicated their lives to us. I know whenever I say "I'm going to the home for a visit," I truly feel every aspect of going home.

I hope you enjoy the following stories in my "walk down memory lane." The stories and poems represent my fondest recollections during a special time, a special place, surrounded by so much history. Hopefully, you will detect the humor, the love, and the wholesome care that helped mold so many lives and fill each of us with our own priceless memories.

THE SURROGATE PLACE

It was Sunday and visitation day at the home. I thought I would get used to the sights and sounds of children greeting their loved ones by now, but I guess, that will never happen. On this particular Sunday, I was feeling very alone and in desperate need of a hug. I would have accepted a hug from anyone. It was a horrible realization to face but I would never be on the receiving end of parental love. There would not be any hugs from relatives on this day.

I walked down the steps of the home's entrance way and out of the wide glass doors. I stomped down the winding sidewalk with a sole determination to get rid of the self—loathing that seemed to consume my thoughts. The summer heat was stifling and the mid-June air hung heavy. The scent of freshly cut grass was laced with a mixture of honeysuckle and roses.

I continued my walk past the grotto, on my way to the St. Joseph's shrine. The shrine was situated at the end of the orchard. The apple trees were lush with shiny new leaves, showing a promise of hundreds of apples. I breathed in deeply, loving the smell of fresh cut grass. I noticed how "Old Andy" kept the lawn and bushes magnificently manicured. We were lucky to have Andy work here at the home. He was always just a stone's throw away from all the activities.

It seemed like yesterday that the orchard was covered with snow and the sisters joined the children for a sleigh ride. I smiled at the vision of Sister Bernadette, round as she was, sliding down the hill on a sleigh. An image of Sister Carlotta's surprised face came to mind, when I hit her accidentally with a snowball. I thought I was in big trouble for that one! Suddenly, sister stooped over, and cupping some snow into a ball, she proceeded to throw a snowball right back at me. Her accuracy was much better than mine and before we knew what was happening we had a real snowball fight going on. Snowballs were flying everywhere. The sound of laughter echoed throughout the orchard.

No longer was this a quiet winter's day. All the sisters and children joined together in the fun. What a winter scene we had created!

As I completed my destination to the Shrine I sat quietly staring at the statue of St. Joseph. I realized that this very quiet spot wasn't visited very often by the other children. The birds loved to sit on St. Joseph's shoulder while chirping a happy tune. How sweet and beautiful the different birds were. The stones that created the shrine were covered with delicate moss that seated the most delicate pastel flowers. This very spot was Sister Gilbert's favorite place. I started to understand why. If any of the children had to find Sister Gilbert, for any reason, this would be the first place to look.

I walked up the flag-stone steps and took a shortcut that led to the ball field. The ball field seemed massive to me. My thoughts were not of the ball field but of the many Easter egg hunts that were enjoyed in these fields by the smaller children. It was an absolute joy for the older children to color the Easter eggs and hide them for the smaller children to hunt.

Gosh, I remember when I was one of the smaller children trying to find the colorful prizes. I started remembering the lazy afternoons when ball practice would be held. Half of the children, myself included, opted to lie in the grassy fields instead of playing ball. We watched the shiny airplanes go by in the sky making a beautiful contrast against the clear blue of the sky. We would sit in the grass for hours tying clover blossoms together making bracelets and necklaces to adorn ourselves with.

As my gaze wandered from the ball field, I spotted the laundry facility and immediately my thoughts stirred. I walked into that building many times to do my chores. The laundry room held three huge washing machines and dryers. There were two oversized presses where bigger items like linens and sheets would be pressed. To the side of the presses was a row of basins used to starch items. Mainly items that were worn by the Sisters...What a tedious job that was. You would immerse the item into the starch basin then hang the item for shaping. Lord, help you if you put too much starch in one of the sister's habits.

The sisters wore starched habits that were heart shaped. This heart framed their lovely faces. A starched bow was attached to the habit and tied directly under their chin. The white collar of their wool dress was starched also. I could never understand how the Sisters wore those long woolen dresses with all the starched items that adorn them, plus black stockings in the middle of this terrible heat. I'm afraid I would have to pin my dress up and tuck it into my waist band and definitely get rid of all those starched items!

There was a room in the back of the main laundry area where ironing boards stood just waiting for someone to press the many baskets of clothing that were deposited under each board. Could you imagine the ironing that had to be done? Somehow I never minded that job because Sister Margaret would let us listen to our choice of music on the radio while we ironed. Boy! What a hot place that was!

I started walking down a different path and decided to take a little rest under one of the shade trees. Thinking of all that heat made me tired. I sat with my legs outstretched staring at the pavilion. During the picnic days the German band would sit under the pavilion and play tunes for hours. How the band blended in the sheer delight of the occasion.

I loved the um-pa-pa sound of the bright brass instruments. The musicians wore the traditional German attire dark green shorts held up with bright red suspenders. Off-white knee-hi stockings made a beautiful contrast with the shorts. Feathered caps adorned their heads. I always thought the feather in the cap resembled a gentleman's shaving brush. Visitors danced the entire day to the band's jolly tunes. Children clapped and sang the words to each and every song.

Across from the pavilion stood a long, inviting wading pool. This pool served as a cool release from the hot summer days. The sisters would let the children take turns wading and running in the cool water. A tall sprinkler in the very center of the pool would rotate and spin as it splashed the children standing nearby. The pool was only a foot deep but that was just enough water for the children to enjoy. No one supervising the pool area ever came away dry.

Within a couple of yards from the wading pool, stood the gymnasium. The skating rink was located directly under the gym. We spent many hours shooting baskets or learning skating techniques at the rink. Both of my brothers were quite good basketball players. During the winter months the boys would host basketball tournaments with nearby schools participating in the games. This kept us all very busy during the cold, winter months.

Upon leaving the gymnasium, I was back on the path from where I started my adventure. I stood for a moment assessing the front entrance way to the home.

The heat was breaking now and parent visitation hours were coming to an end. Somehow, I felt better about the day. A quiet, peaceful walk around the grounds of my home made me feel quite fortunate with the way my life had been destined. I felt secure and comforted with the loving memories of the home that were locked away in my heart.

Dedication of "Child of War" Poem

Writing poetry and short stories has become a passion with me.
It seems to be a mood release which also affects
the way I perceive the order or challenges of life.
Growing up in an orphanage
I have always had a certain urgency
to protect and defend
the children of this world.
Too often, the children go unprotected.
This poem addresses the characteristics
of a child as he
experiences the "Wars of Life."
Children deserve to be innocent and happy.
All children deserve our trust and our love.

***

Child of War

Why a frown on this child who is so forlorn and down?
What has this poor child seen?
To make his eyes so sad while cast down
hiding his tears
that seep slowly to the ground.
What is it that formed a pool of such sadness and fear?
What robbed this innocent heart of its childish years?
When laughter used to be the light—
that poured forth from his very sight
and hidden smiles could never stay his soul.
It will take many years of gentle embrace
to try and erase the fears, the hurt, and the anger.
It will take a heart full of love
to bring this lovely dove
the peace and trust of others.
If time could take away his mournful memories

and mankind could make him feel secure.
If together we could make him want—once again,
to feel, to touch, to believe, and to trust
To give all that is certain and should rightfully be...
his total dependence on us!

A VERY SPECIAL CRUISE

I was about five when my grandfather sent a note to the Sisters saying that he would like to treat the children in the orphan home to a day on the Admiral Steamer Boat. I can't remember how many children were to take part on this excursion but I remember being so excited that I almost made myself sick. My brothers were very excited too because we seldom saw our grandfather. We knew Grandpa was a very important man because he was the Captain of that particular boat.

The morning of the cruise was glorious. It was sunny and hot, a perfect day in July to be on the water. Sister Zita dressed me in my finest dress. It was one of my favorites. It was red and white striped with little puffy see-through sleeves and a matching see-through collar. Down the front of the dress were tiny rounded buttons continuing to the waist. Sister Zita was my kindergarten teacher and surrogate mother for the time. She had a crooked pointer finger, and I realize now how buttoning all those tiny buttons on my dress must have almost "done her in."

The children boarded the buses for the outing, and as usual in those days, the boys were on one bus and the girls were on the other. Thinking back to those days, the boy/girl separation included all things. The orphan home was divided into two sides, boys' and girls' living quarters. The playground had an imaginary line that no one dared to cross. You just knew which side was the boys' side and which side was the girls' side and the separation continued. The entrance to the home and the chapel were all in the center of the home or as I liked to say "the heart of the home." We did take our meals with our siblings though. Each family would sit together at an assigned table. Usually, this was one of the favorite times of the day, for all the boys and girls.

I don't remember much of the bus ride to the boat; I just remember feeling very happy to see my grandpa and my grandma. You see, Grandma worked on the boat also. Her job was selling hot dogs and ice cream. She always worked with Grandpa. They came together from their home in New Orleans where they worked on the St. Paul boat. When the owners of the Admiral decided to bring the boat to St. Louis, Grandma and Grandpa came too. This is when St. Louis became my family home.

Sister Zita led the procession of children from the buses to the boat. It was something to see the line of children as they paraded down the brick laden path leading to the muddy waters and the beautiful silver boat that awaited their fun-filled adventure.

There were many people on the boat watching as the children boarded. I was in awe of everything. I couldn't imagine anything being so big or so pretty. The first floor where we boarded the boat was filled with concession stands, games, tables and chairs. This is where my grandma worked. I didn't know where she was at the moment. She didn't make her presence known. We made our way to the second floor, and up a grand stairway. Thick green and purple carpet filled the steps that led to a beautiful wooden dance floor with a stage set-up for a live "big" band.

As we made our way to the top deck, I could hear music bellowing from an instrument called a calliope. This looked very similar to an organ except the calliope had pipes that would bellow when you struck its keys. What a grand sound the calliope made. You felt like dancing and singing to every tune and it certainly put a smile on everyone's face.

People were standing everywhere on the top deck of the boat looking out at the mighty Mississippi with its foaming waves and the magnificent view of downtown St. Louis. Sister Zita tapped my shoulder and I followed the direction of her pointed finger. There, in what they called the pilot house stood my grandpa. He looked so very handsome in his captain's uniform. His complete attire was immaculate. One would say he looked perfect. He donned a white hat with a shiny black brim and the small glasses on his nose were so clean they mirrored the instrument panel located directly in front of him.

What a sight! I'll never forget! I really didn't know my grandpa very well but I do believe my brothers knew him a little better than I. I wasn't even sure that he would know who I was. Sister Zita instructed me to stand very quietly by the boat railing while she had a few words with my Grandpa. Sister pointed timidly in my direction and my grandfather's gaze rested upon my tiny frame. I hoped my dress looked pretty to him and I prayed my wild curly hair didn't look too messy. I just wanted him to like me.

Grandpa motioned for me to come to him. I must have looked like my shoes were glued to the very spot where I was standing. My feet wouldn't move and my palm wouldn't let go of the railing. He motioned again and this time Grandpa smiled. That smile was all it took for me to run up to him and throw my small arms around his neck.

Grandpa took me into the pilot house and showed me the instruments that were needed to run his big boat. He let me touch the handle that signaled to start up the engines. I peered out the windows of the pilot house and could see all the people standing around waiting for the blast from the enormous horn that proclaimed the cruise was on its way. I couldn't stop looking at my grandpa as he gave the command to start the engines and start the cruise. He was so very perfect in every way. If given the chance I would have stayed right there in that pilot house with my grandpa and my brothers forever.

Grandpa walked us down to the first floor to see our grandma. I could see the curious glances of the other passengers as we walked by them with our grandpa. I felt like I was walking in a palace and Grandpa was the king.

Grandma was very glad to see my brothers and myself. She gave us ice cream and hot dogs and we all danced to the music of the big band while we visited and talked. Grandma was dressed in a uniform too. Her uniform wasn't as handsome as grandpa's was but she sure looked important too!

It seemed that we had just started the cruise and already it was time for it to end. This would be the end of a wonderful, unforgettable journey. Sister Zita took my hand once again as I said my farewell to my grandpa and grandma. I thanked them for the wonderful day and hoped that there would be more days like this ahead. Slowly, the parade of children began to exit the boat, only to board the buses that awaited our delivery back to the home. I spent hours that night thinking of my grandpa and grandma. I felt so happy to have had a special day with them. I couldn't help feeling a little hurt though because I never understood why I couldn't live on the boat with them. It was only a few short weeks after our big day on the boat, when the news of my grandpa's death sadly took a slice from my tiny heart. Grandpa had a heart attack while on one of his daily excursions down the Mississippi. Sister Zita said, "At least it happened while he was doing the thing he loved to do." She was right, you know, the boat was what Grandpa loved. It was his life. He really didn't do anything else but cruise on down the river. I guess there was something magical to him, in the way the river found its course together with the big steamer boat.

I prayed that Grandpa would be in peace now. I will always remember that wonderful and very special day that he gave to us children. The laughter, the fun, the excitement we all shared will be etched forever in my heart as we shared in Grandpa's pride of his shiny, beautiful boat.

A LESSON LEARNED

My older brother Jerry was instructed, by one of the sisters, to remove a lump from my head which he had angrily placed there. He was told that he had exactly thirty minutes to make this disappearing act happen.

One evening, while sitting at the supper table, I was filled with the dickens and in a very chipper mood. You might say, "I was feeling my muscles." You know how it is when you just feel like you can take on the world and nobody can tell you what to do? Well, that is the scenario of one particular cold October evening. I was about six years old and just learning how to use my knife for cutting and for spreading purposes. One other tidbit of information I should fess up to is-—my nickname at the time was "butterball" because I had an insatiable appetite for butter. To get on with the story, I decided that I could spread my own bread without anyone's help. This included either of my brothers or the sisters.

My eldest brother Jerry was feeling in a "don't mess around with me" mood, which didn't particularly go along with the mood I was in. One might call this an explosive situation.

As I was about to grab for the butter dish, Jerry said, "I'll spread your butter bread."

I replied emphatically "I don't need you or anyone else to spread my bread. I can do it all by myself." With these words scarcely out of my mouth, I lunged forward with knife in hand and scooped up half of the butter from the tub. I plunked the butter precariously onto the bread then started to giggle. I thought how clever I was to place so much butter on my bread with just one stab of the knife.

My brother Bobby was giggling too and said, "Let me help you, Sis…that is way too much butter on your bread." With Bobby as an ally, I became even sillier.

"Don't touch my bread, Bobby. I can eat this and the rest of the butter in the tub too." The giggling continued, only louder. I stabbed the other half of the butter from the tub and placed it, very neatly I might add, next to the other hunk of butter still hunkering on the edge of my bread.

Jerry had enough of this foolishness. "Put the butter back in the tub and let me help you spread the bread the right way," he yelled.

"I can do it myself," I said. The look on my older brother's face was a definite warning for me not to carry on with this silly business but I was feeling on top of the world and very defiant.

With a flash of anger, and a gleam in my big brother's eye that I will never forget, he lunged forward. The "speed of lightning" saying didn't start with Superman…It started with the "speed of lightning" that my brother displayed as he grabbed the knife from my hand and with the heavy-handle part of the knife he whacked me a good one—right on the top of my head. I was so surprised, hurt and amazed all at the same time that I didn't even realize the blood curdling sound that tore from deep within my throat.

Sister Louietrout, who was the nun on duty in the dining room, came running. She was a rather round sister but just as tall as she was round. She pulled my brother from his chair and then came around the table to collect me. We were both pulled into the kitchen and placed in front of the sink. With one quick gulp, the instructions were stated, "You, Sir, will get several pieces of ice from the freezer and grab a washrag. You will then remove that lump from your sister's head which you angrily placed there. This disappearing act will happen before the evening vespers or else."

Well, we knew that vespers were recited by the nuns, promptly at 7:00 p.m. in the small chapel. We almost panicked as Sister Louietrout turned and slammed the door behind her as she hurriedly walked back to the dining room. If supper was served at 6:00 p.m. then we only had approximately thirty minutes to remove this huge lump from my head.

I started to back away from my brother as tears streamed down my cheeks. "How are you going to remove this lump from my head Jerry?" I asked.

Jerry's eyes softened as he realized the hurt and fear that shown on my face. "Come here, Sis, we will have to press real hard on the lump with the ice," he said. "I'm sorry I hurt you, but you need to ask for help and not be such a ninny at times." I looked up at Jerry and saw the love and concern showing on his face. At that particular moment I would have taken a hundred lumps on the head and all the pain in the world just to have my big brother look at me like that. Anyway, I was enjoying spending this little extra time with my big brother while everyone else had to go back to their rooms.

A short time later, Sister Louietrout came back into the kitchen to see if the lump was removed from my head. To her surprise, though the tears were still streaming down my face, the lump in question had tremendously decreased in size. She saw how my brother was lovingly holding my head as he applied the ice and her heart melted just as quickly as the ice in his hand. Sister let us visit for a few more minutes and then we had to hurry back to join the other children. No more punishments would be handed out since we were able to make the lump disappear.

Once outside of the kitchen, I reached up and hugged a surprised nun. I whispered, "Thank you Sister, for giving me more time with my big brother and for showing him how to get rid of that painful lump."

Sister Louietrout hugged me for a brief moment, then swished me off to my room. Sister continued walking down the hall making sure not to be too late for her vespers.

SACRAMENT PREPARATION

The tulips were showing off their magnificent colors as the daffodils swayed like dancing bonnets in the wind. Spring was here and this spring would start off like none I had ever experienced. This spring I would pledge my heart and soul to my God.

I would be dressed in white just like a bride. That is what my third grade teacher said, as we discussed the sacrament of First Holy Communion. This very important act would require months of preparation and excitement for my entire class.

Confession is a sacrament too, which you receive before your First Communion. It is a time when you take a hard look into yourself and think of all the bad acts or bad deeds that you have committed. While thinking of all the bad things, it is then the time to express sorrow for the evil doings by reciting the Act of Contrition. This way you tell the Lord out loud that you will try to be a better person and you truly are sorry for what you have done to offend Him.

Before you receive the body of Jesus, in First Holy Communion, you would have to make your first confession.

Now, the thought of telling someone my bad deeds and explaining the sins I committed, just terrified me to death. I wanted to be a part of the Communion with all my heart but I wasn't too sure about telling all in confession.

In class sister gave us practice sheets for confession. This way we wouldn't be afraid of forgetting our sins...if we wrote them down. We wouldn't panic when it came time to tell our priest in the confessional about our bad deeds.

We wrote, on our practice sheet, the different sins that sister had previously written on the blackboard. She explained the different sins to us and how they were a part of evil. I wrote all the big words next to the small ones. I already knew what some of the sins were but never understood some of the other big sins like adultery and fornication. I knew that I was guilty of telling a few lies or sneaking food to another child's plate. I stuck my tongue out at Sister Florence when she wasn't looking and I gave the bad finger sign, with my pinky finger, when Sister Robert made me stay after school to do math homework. My older brother Bobby was real good at giving that pinky finger to other people but that was his sin not mine.

I'm pretty good now at saying all the prayers. I'm a master at the Act of Contrition prayer, too. This prayer is said in the confessional after you tell father your sins and he asks, "Are you sorry for your sins?" You answer, "Yes," and then he says, "Say the Act of Contrition and the Lord will forgive you, my child."

We had to stand up at teacher's desk and say the Act of Contrition out loud for all the class to hear. This way Sister Florence knew if you were ready for the big sacrament or not. Well, I think I surprised sister and everyone in the class because I knew that prayer by heart. I studied very hard for this day.

Time for our first confession arrived. Wouldn't you believe it, we were having a visiting priest from the neighboring parish. Oh well, this was good because I could take my practice sheet into the confessional and read the little sins to father. He wouldn't know me and he wouldn't think I was so bad. I wondered how many Hail Mary's and Our Father prayers he would give me for my evil doings?

As I stood in line for my turn in the confessional, I glanced at my classmates to see if anyone was going to act silly, or flip out or do any other kind of dumb thing. Everyone was very contrite. I stopped looking at my classmates and started to peer into the eyes of the statue situated directly in front of me. It was a statue of Mary, the mother of Jesus, holding her son in her arms. Of course, I entered into my usual emotional self. I didn't want to be a sinner. I wanted to be the best child that lived in the orphan home. I wanted Jesus and His mother to be proud of me so one day they would welcome me into their home in heaven. I knew I was going to heaven because I didn't commit hardly any of those horrible sins that sister talked about in class.

My turn to enter the confessional was at hand. My palms started sweating and for some reason I had to fight for control as tears tried to claim the moment. Its ok I told myself, I don't even know the priest in there.

I knelt on the padded kneeler, made the sign of the cross and uttered the correct words, "Bless me father, this is my first confession." I was on a roll now.

Father asked, "Tell me child what sins have you committed?"

Sins? What sins? My lips were dry and I was frozen to the spot. Father whispered again, "What sins have you committed, child?"

I suddenly pulled out my practice sheet with shaky hands and began reading. I read this sheet so many times that I practically memorized all the sins on it. All the big and the little sins. "I committed adultery three times, I said. I also coveted my neighbor's goods, at least four times." The list continued and I felt as if it were growing.

Finally, Father said with a knowing voice. "Are you sorry for those terrible sins my child?"

"Yes, I repeated."

Then Father asked me to recite the Act of Contrition. I know this, I said to myself. Why can't I remember it? Father said, "its ok honey, I'll help you." I repeated the prayer after Father as he had suggested. Finally, father told me to say one Our Father and one Hail Mary and all was forgiven.

I left the confessional feeling on top of the world. He only gave me one Our Father and one Hail Mary. That wasn't bad for the first time. I knelt at the church pew and said my prayers with all the earnestness I could muster.

I promise never to do those evil sins again. I hoped with all my heart that Father wouldn't know that I was the one that had just recited from my practice sheet. I did remember to state at the very end of all my sins—sometimes I cheated. That way, if saying my practice sheet was cheating, then I would be forgiven.

The following Sunday we dressed in our beautiful First Communion attire. The white of my dress cast a shimmery glow from the sun as it shone through the hall window. As we stood in a single-file line preparing to make our entrance into the chapel, I was thrilled to the bone. I felt like a new bride waiting for Sister Gilbert's signal for us to begin our procession. Her choir of angels sang a specially selected song and I felt so clean and holy for that moment.

The sisters gave each of the children a rosary as a gift to remember this most sacred day. I held my rosary tight in my hands as we processed down the center aisle of the chapel. I glanced at Sister Florence to make sure I was doing all that a proper First Communicant was supposed to be doing. I would not make a mistake today!

My brother Jerry was assisting Father with mass as an Altar boy at this grand celebration. I felt so happy and proud as the time drew near for us children to receive our precious Jesus for the first time. We processed once again to the communion rail and knelt down. The choir sang a beautiful song about the body and blood of Jesus. The sun filled the chapel as the stained glass windows displayed a magnificent shower of color on the altar. My brother Jerry held the pallet by my neck, just in case Father missed my tongue that was extended. We wouldn't want the host to fall to the ground. That would be disgraceful. I closed my eyes as father laid the host on my tongue. I held the host in my mouth for a few moments and then swallowed remembering not to chew. I walked back to my pew and knelt reverently once again as I spoke my heart's words to Jesus.

As mass ended, Father stated, "Go in peace my children." The first communicants walked back down the aisle making their grand exit. Once again, the choir of sisters sang "Hallelujah." I knew I would never be the same. I knew I would be closer to heaven and I felt that I really belonged here, in this most holy chapel of God.

THE STORY TELLER

Father Edgar Ryan was the pastor of the home when I was a very small child. He was in the priestly order of the Jesuit's; therefore, his attire was quite different than that of the usual priest. Father could be seen roaming the grounds in a long priestly gown called a cassock. His feet sported sandals with no socks. Father had a round bald spot on top of his head and I never knew if that was his normal hair line or part of his priestly garb. He was usually seen puffing on a short round cigar that he referred to as his stogie. This was so uncharacteristic of a priest. Sometimes his stogie would be lit and other times he just kind of chewed on the end of it. It didn't look very good but I sort of liked the way the stogie smelled when father lit it and then sat puffing away on it. It was neat the way the smoke would twirl around Father's head making him look as though he had a halo. Sometimes we children would yell, "hey father can you make circles with your smoke?" Well, he would huff and puff and then by making his mouth form a perfect circle he blew smoke creating perfect circles everywhere. He was simply amazing. If one would pretend not to like the smell of smoke, he would take a deep puff and blow the smoke in your face. I hated that, but loved the attention of being singled out as he blew the smoke my way. It was an attention getter for many children.

Father Edgar, as we called him, made a daily game out of selecting one of the girls to wear his beautiful paper ring. The ring was really a cigar band but we liked to pretend it was the real thing. Father saved the bands just knowing he would play this special game and bring a smile to many faces. Everything father did was in fun for father enjoyed visiting with us children. He used to say to us, "Children, you certainly are my therapy." And you know what? He was good therapy for us too!

One afternoon Father made his usual entrance onto the playground. He waved to all the children then he parked his huge frame on one of the picnic benches. The children surrounded him with shouts of glee. We waited to see just what Father was up to. All of us already knew his exact routine. We knew that once Father was seated, he would then loosen his white starched collar, and after that, a hush would settle over the crowd-for a story was about to be told. You see, Father was an avid story teller. We would sit and listen to him for hours with his deep baritone voice. I'll bet the sisters loved when Father made his presence known for it surely afforded them a much deserved break.

My memory wanders to a special summer day when Father took his seat and proceeded through his usual routine. Suddenly, he pointed in my direction and said, "Today, children, we will hear the story about Ruth". I was so excited by this good news. I was the only child in the home with this name.

I never gave it much thought as to where the name came from or what special meaning it might hold. I did know that my real mother and father gave me this name. I never knew if they had a reason for it though. Could it belong to my Dad's grandmother or mother? Or maybe I had a great aunt named Ruth or maybe they had someone else in mind that was special to them. I really didn't care anyway. I didn't give much thought to my name before now.

Father told a magical tale. Ruth married a man named Boaz and she worked hard by his side. She worked in the fields and harvested grain. She was widowed at an early age and took care of her mother-in-law. Father explained that Ruth was a Hebrew name. It had a special meaning known to all as the "faithful one." Ruth lived up to her name. She was the loyal daughter—in—law of Ann. Ann was the great grandmother of the infant child, Jesus. Father spoke on and on. As I listened, I felt a contentment settle over me. I was so honored to be named after someone so good and gentle.

The story came to its conclusion and Father Edgar grasped my small thin hand in his large strong hand. Unexpectedly, he slipped his paper band on my ring finger. "Now you know child. Your name is special and so are you. You must always remember your story and live as your namesake has lived. Love God and honor those around you." I knew at that moment that Father Edgar had stolen a little piece of my heart. He brought me a certain pride to my name and caused strength to fill my soul. I knew that I would always live up to the purpose of my name. I was proud to be called Ruth, the faithful one. What a strong name. I promised there on that spot that I would always be faithful to anyone who loved me. I would never leave or hurt anyone. I wondered if my mom or dad knew what strength I found in the special name that they gave me. That is one thing I will always be grateful to them for. my name.

HEARTS MEND TOGETHER

During the holidays most of the children enjoyed going home for a visit with their parents, aunts and uncles, or grandparents. Visitation to the orphan home was usually held on the fourth Sunday of every month. All visits took place in the home's auditorium, where most get-togethers usually occurred.

My brothers and I seldom had a visitor. It was too hard for our grandmother to visit us since she didn't have any driving skills and she worked most of her time on the Admiral steamer boat, taking cabs back and forth to and from work. Grandmother loved her steamer boat and, after Grandpa's death, that was how she made it through her lonely days. Her loneliness was soon consumed by working longer hours and extended days on the boat. That was her life and, God love her, she needed something.

I often liked to think she could find Grandpa's spirit there on that boat. Grandpa and Grandma both worked together and loved their life as "river people."

Grandma's free week-ends were spent visiting our mother, who was institutionalized with a mental illness. I never realized before what a sad life that Grandma must have had.

I often spent nights in wonderment about my family and what they were doing. I'd try to imagine what life was like on the outside of the home's walls but really never knew or understood what happened in a normal family situation outside of the home. Sometimes imagination is a blessed thing; often it can be cruel and hurting. You see, I was gifted with an imagination that seemed to magnify and taunt me with age.

Watching my friends dress for visitors didn't bother me for years. But soon, as I grew a little older, it became harder to be left behind. I watched the excitement and profound hysteria as one child after another heard their name called for visitation.

It seemed that the few of us who didn't receive visitors were guarded very carefully by the sisters. We were kept busy at least until the first hour of visitation had proceeded into the next. The sisters always referred to idleness as the devil's workshop. Keep busy and your imagination will not run away with you. That is what they would say!

It was getting harder to be contained in the lounge of our dorm while waiting for my friends to return from their visits. I wanted to hear their news and the outcome of their visits.

It wasn't long before curiosity would overcome me. On these days imagination was not my friend. I wanted to see Bethy's mom and Patricia's father. I needed to see if Natalie's grandfather would be nice to her and love her or shun her again with his hurtful words.

I certainly could understand why Natalie was not permitted to live with him. He could be so crude at times. If Bethy's mom started crying again, I could be there to help Bethy and maybe keep her from crying. She always cried for days after her mother's visit. Gosh, I think Bethy was made with a tear dysfunction.

I walked down to the auditorium where the visits were taking place. It wasn't hard to get away from the dorm. Sister Paul was so busy with her sewing I knew just when to escape, especially when it was time to rip out another hem.

Before my foot hit the last step I could hear the rumble of voices and the shouts of excited children as they laughed merrily with their loved ones. On occasion I would witness a friend cry or wail to return home with their family. I would see mothers soothingly brush the hair back from their child's face or a dad who lovingly patted his son's knee while talking in deep tones.

Other but similar scenes were repeated as I glanced around the room. It was unreal to me that some families had a separation of children. Some lived at the home while others were still with their parents. I never understood why all the children were not together. I guess some parents had too many problems to take care of everyone. I did know that Theresa could not live at home because of something her daddy did. The boys were still at home but not Theresa. As I glanced from one group of visitors to another my eyes rested on a lady standing in the vestibule. She was looking around like she was lost. I'll never understand why my imagination kicked in at that particular moment, but it did.

Standing there was my loving mother with her arms out stretched to me and an incredible smile reached every contour of her face. I proceeded to make my way toward this lovely image and for just a few but wonderful moments, I was overcome with a peace and love that I had never before experienced. My walk turned into a run as I quickly approached this vision called Mother.

I didn't see my friend Barbara walking down the steps to greet her Aunty Mae. I often heard Barbara talk about her pretty aunt who would come and visit occasionally but I never had the opportunity to meet her.

Before Barbara could reach her aunt my arms surrounded her in the tightest bear-like grip that could only be broken by Barbara's heart wrenching words..."Aunty Mae." I looked up into the most astonishing blue eyes I had ever seen. Truly this was Barbara's aunt for there in the image of her beautiful eyes were the same color eyes of my dear friend's eyes.

Embarrassment and hurt immediately flowed through me as I ran for the only place where I could find solace and peace. I ran to the chapel , "The Heart of the Home." I often came to the chapel when I was threatened by uncontrollable tears. Here, I could talk out my problems in complete seclusion without anyone hearing me. Here I didn't have to feel the presence of visiting day. I didn't have to see the hugs and love that were not meant for me.

I cried and prayed fervently to the Blessed Mother Mary. After all, she was my Mother and would protect me from this hurtful moment. I would pray with all my heart for her to fold me into her breast, wrap me in her mantle of blue. There I would be warm, comfortable and loved. As always, after a good cry—I proceeded to fall into a deep sleep.

Sister Marie was the guardian angel of the chapel. I loved to work with her. She always spoke softly and hummed in perfect unison as her hands folded the linens for the altar. When visiting hours were over for the Sunday, Sister Paul never panicked when I was nowhere to be found. She knew that I would be returned in the arms of my guardian angel from the chapel.

She knew where I usually ended up on visiting days. She also knew that the heart of the orphan home soothed my own aching heart and, as always, the morning would bring a smile back to my lips and another whirlwind of excitement would take over as my never ending imagination would beckon yet another day's activity.

HAND IN HAND

Mother Superior thought it was time for my brothers and I to meet our real mother. We knew that mother lived in a mental hospital and had to be watched by nurses at all times. None of us looked forward to this meeting, nor did we understand what would come from this visitation. Sister explained that there would be plenty of people around to look after us and so we would be safe. The visit would be short and necessary.

The halls were painted with a drab white on top and green on the bottom. Bars lined the windows and doors. Going to see my real mother was a horror of emotions at the age of nine. My brothers and I didn't know our mother. We only knew stories about her. Mother and father were just words one might say, but never feel as a human touch or presence. My father had been gone for a long time, since I was the mere age of one.

The ride on the bus to the hospital was a long and anxious process. We, the children of the home that is, never left the orphanage much. If we did leave, it was always in the company of an adult and usually for the purpose of some fun-filled event. I didn't like this whole visitation episode and prayed for the strength to get through the day. The one thing I did like about this day was spending time with my brothers. Apparently, they weren't in the best of moods either. This was just one of those "hope it gets over," days.

My feet were frozen to the spot of the hallway after leaving the elevator. We were on mother's floor. A gate was blocking our entrance to the hall where mother lived. The guard on the elevator told us, "Ring the bell to the left of the doorway and someone will let you pass." I couldn't reach the bell but my older brother could. He rang and within seconds the heavy, rusted gate opened to a world I never knew existed.

My knees almost buckled as I held tight to my brother's hands. Jerry, who was the eldest, stood on the right of me, and Bobby, who is four years older than me, stood to the left. I could tell that they were just as scared as I was. We took a seat at one of the tables in a room that the nurse had guided us into. There were people everywhere. Some were sitting and smoking cigarettes, one was dancing without a partner, and another one was twirling her hair around her finger as she drew imaginary circles on the wall. I felt an eerie chill across my back and hoped that the time to leave would come soon. The nurse brought my mother to us. I'll never forget the way she looked. She was tiny, only 4 feet 11 inches tall. She had auburn hair that hung loose around her face and very sad green eyes. "She's really quite beautiful," I thought. I fought the urge to run up to her and wrap my arms around her in a hug because I was so afraid. I didn't know what she would do or how she would react to such an action. She really didn't say much. She just glided into the chair next to mine.

We all sat together when suddenly I reached up to hold her hand. I looked at her hand and I could see that it wasn't shaking but I could feel her shaking. It felt like she had a vibrator inside of her hand. As I looked up into her tender face she smiled then she spoke quietly to my brothers. As she turned in my direction, she cupped my face in her small, shaking hands. "My baby," she said to me.

I'll never forget that simple gesture. I was so wrapped up with emotion that my eyes stung with tears that burned for release. I waited for such a long time to hear such tender words from my mother. I knew that no matter what, she loved me.

My mind was reeling, but with all that was going on I didn't notice the commotion in the room. A couple of patients had a disagreement and started to fight. Movement of chairs and bodies were happening everywhere. The nurse pulled me away from my mother. Without so much as a goodbye, my brothers and I were ushered down the hallway and escorted to the elevators. We were on our way out of the hospital. I didn't get the chance to ask mother any questions or tell her that I loved her. The dam of tears that had been held back, with so much emotion, began to gush down my face. I looked up at my brothers and saw that tears stained their faces too. Once again we clasped hands together with Jerry on my right and Bobby on my left. We boarded the bus with one last glance at the hospital. I tried to look up at the windows thinking maybe I would get one last glimpse of my mother but saw nothing. Never again would I want to spend a day like this one. I couldn't get back to the home fast enough.

I ran into the waiting arms of Sister Paul. Tears fell once again as she tried to soothe away the hurt and pain. I knew she would make the hurt go away. How could I ever manage life without my dear sisters?

WORTH A WHACK

L ife was very different as a young girl growing up in an orphan home. Instead of parents we had nuns, or Sisters, often referred to as "Stirs," a shortened name that was placed in front of their given name. For instance, Sister Marie would be shortened to Stir Marie. This was a very common practice for the children in the home.

Once a month the "Stirs" would surprise us with a movie in the auditorium. This was a special treat for being good. We would all gather excitedly, girls on one side of the auditorium and boys on the other side. The Stirs would keep the title of the movie a secret until it lit up the screen. One thing we knew for sure was it would be a fun-filled night.

One particular Saturday the feature movie shown was, "Tarzan The Ape Man." Wow! Was I impressed! I fell deeply in love with this character, Tarzan. Imagine, a handsome man with flesh exposed swinging from tree to tree in a loin cloth. I realized at that very moment—I would always favor Tarzan movies the rest of my life. The only sound you could hear in the auditorium was the "Stirs" as they shook their starched habits from side to side and made sounds of "Oh, My," and "Oh, Boy."

Well, after the movie had ended, it was getting quite late in the evening. We were instructed to go quietly to our dormitories and change into our pajamas. This was to be done in a quiet manner acting in our usual ladylike behavior. Sure, right, we were going to do all this after viewing Tarzan!

I do believe I was one of the first girls to start the commotion, as I rolled up my pajama legs, and jumped from bed to bed in a fashion that Tarzan would have been so proud of. I tested my lungs in the most un-lady like fashion as I began to yell the jungle chant that was all so famous in the Tarzan movies.

Stir Florence appeared out of no where! Her face was as red as a beet. It took just one small second for us to realize we had all sealed our fate. Girls scrambled in every direction trying to locate their beds. We tried to hide the laughter that was echoing uncontrollably throughout the dormitory. We all knew we were doomed! Stir Florence picked up one of the radiator brushes from a nearby wall and began to whack our individual behinds. I never saw Sister so upset! When it came to my turn, Tarzan was still totally on my mind. I thought for sure that Stir was getting tired from all that whacking and I was still filled with the dickens. Once again, I couldn't resist letting out the famous Tarzan yell, another whack, which only stirred yet another Tarzan yell. I was determined that no one on this particular night would break my newly found spirit.

Finally, Stir Florence gave up and left the room with the expectation that we would all quietly cry ourselves to sleep. "That will put an end to all this silliness," she stated while making her exit. I knew she had to have been completely exhausted. It wasn't long after Sister departed when one snicker started after another. Soon, all the girls were joining in complete belly laughter.

If one dared to put their ear close to the dormitory door and listen, I bet they would hear Stir Florence snickering on the other side of the door as she huffed and puffed trying to catch her breath. I'm also quite sure she was very tempted to try the all famous jungle chant herself!

MY DEAR FRIEND, TINA

Sister Clarisse came down to the playroom and summoned me and two other girls to follow her. Tina, Bethy, Barbara and I were about 10 years old. We were in the same grade, same dorm and best of friends. We walked down a long corridor on our way to the infirmary. After a while the walls in the hallway seemed to close-in on me. I found myself wondering if my friend Tina was getting any better or had she gotten worse? I've never seen anyone as sick as Tina. Have you ever heard of people saying, "She's turning green"? Well, I know first hand what that means. Tina was green, gray and sweaty before they took her away from us. She had a terrible cough and was very weak.

While on chore duty in the chapel, I would find myself looking up at the window of the infirmary. When children were sick or had to be isolated because of illness they would be sent to the infirmary. While in the infirmary the children could still see and hear the daily mass through a beautiful stained glass window that overlooked the chapel. It was higher than any window in the home. I wished Tina would look out of the window at me so I could tell her to get well.

As we approached near the infirmary door, Sister Clarisse turned in one large swoop. She placed her finger on her lips as if to hush us, but I really don't believe a sound could be heard from any of us, except for the pounding of our hearts. How do you quiet your heart?

Sister Clarisse started talking in a very low voice. She explained to us that Tina was very, very ill and wanted to see her best friends. She was so restless that the doctor thought it would be best to summon us girls and let us visit our sick friend. If this was the only way to get her to rest, then we would have to be called. I said to Sister in a whisper," I don't want to get sick, but I miss Tina so much that by gosh, I'll not worry about getting sick." Besides, we could make Tina laugh. We were her buddies and knew the things that would make her smile. Doesn't that take care of everything?

As we entered the infirmary, Sister Robert was standing by Tina's bed. Sister was dressed all in white. She had on a white apron, white gloves, and a white veil. My eyes were starting to blur at all the white I saw. The lights were low and I felt the hair on the back of my neck stand up. My palms were sweaty and if I could turn around, I knew I would be right out that door, making my way down the corridor. All I could think of at the moment was getting away.

I didn't like the smell of the room and there just wasn't any air to breathe. All too suddenly my attention was jerked back to my friend, Tina, as she whispered my name. I heard it just as plain as if Sister Clarisse called me. Tina wasn't moving and I walked to the bedside.

Her hair was wet and pushed off her forehead. Tina always wore bangs. She just didn't look the same. She was as pale as I've ever seen and her eyes—I will never forget how shiny and glassy they looked as she peered right through me. I tried to smile but my lips just wouldn't move; they were so dry. No words formed from my mouth. I just stood there looking at Tina while holding her hand. She knew I was there by her side. She knew all of us were there. We were her playmates, her confidants, her friends. I loved her as much as you would love a sister. Funny thing though, I never told her that. Somehow she knew it. She had to know how important she was to the three of us.

Finally, I managed to tell Tina that I set up the Monopoly game for her and I sure needed a partner. She smiled and I knew right then and there that Tina would be all right and soon we would be yelling and laughing and.....Tina started to cough; her breathing was extremely labored.

Suddenly, she started talking to Jesus. She stretched her hands out and called to Jesus just as if he were in the room standing right next to Sister Mary Robert. I have never been so scared in my life. I knew something bad was about to happen. The tears were streaming down my face and I fell to my knees. I could hear Barbara sobbing but not a sound came from Beth. Poor Bethy, she would never survive this. As I glanced from Beth to Barbara my gaze fell on the Crucifix that hung so perfectly centered above Tina's bed. I knew then without being told that within a few short moments Tina would be called to heaven. We would no longer have our dear friend to laugh with or play with. I prayed with all my heart that Tina would be ok but I guess just as Tina called out to Jesus—he heard her call. Jesus was taking Tina to her new home to be with him. I was glad that she wouldn't be sick anymore, but oh how I will miss my dear, dear friend.

As the following years flowed together, I never once forgot my friend—not for a day. Every time I had duty in the chapel or walked back from receiving communion, during morning mass, my gaze would rest upon the highest window of the chapel and I knew my best friend Tina was sitting there smiling at me from above.

My Dear Friend

When I close my eyes I can still see her face
What I would give for one last embrace.
I can see her dark brown eyes
as I swim in the tenderness of their sigh;
Again, I gently stroke my tears away;
and look forward to yet another day.

My gaze rests upon the window
that has kept my friend so far away.
When I look upon the colored glass
my vision is focused on just one thing.

I'm trying to see her shadow, now of the past
is she gazing back at me?
Can she tell me that she's at rest?
Her memories I will cherish forever;
they will become a part of my total being.
Whenever loneliness surrounds me
I'll hold her tight in my secret dreams.

She was born with such goodness;
a treasure so rare was she.
No wonder God so loved her beauty
and took her away from me.

THE MAKE OVER

Shirley Temple was a young movie star who could charm almost anyone that entered her world. She had her own television show that aired every Sunday night. It was called the Shirley Temple Theater. I loved to watch her movies while pretending that I was that shining star. My favorite movie was "Heidi." This was a story about a young girl that was orphaned. She had a lonely grandfather who lived high on the Swiss Alps. She wanted to live with this cantankerous old man who didn't care one dime for anyone. The whole movie was about their relationship and the love that developed between the two of them. My imagination was certainly stirred by this priceless movie. All of Shirley's movies were wonderful.

It was my 8th birthday and I had decided that I would ask Sister for a special request. I wanted Sister Carlotta to make me look just like Shirley Temple. Shirley had beautiful short curly hair and her nose held a spattering of freckles. As I peered into the mirror I could see that I too had a spattering of freckles across my nose. My hair though, was something else. It simply wouldn't do. It was all wrong for this special look. It was straight and very long. The end of my hair hung close to my waist. It had to go. Sister Carlotta listened to my request and stated that my hair was too beautiful. She hated the thought of cutting it off. After all, it was probably one of my best features.

"Are you sure you want to do this, child? " she questioned. "I beg you with all my heart," was my reply. I wanted to look just like Shirley. "I realize that Shirley doesn't wear glasses," I whined. "And she didn't have any missing front teeth either," Sister stated. Still, I knew that if my hair was cut right and curled, then I would resemble that cute little star.

Sister regretfully grabbed for her scissors. I flung my long hair over my shoulder at the same time. Sister slapped at my arm and muttered for me to be still. She said, "If you keep fidgeting around the way you are right now, you might just end up bald." I decided to sit very still and let sister perform her best. Sister also bought a new product just for this special occasion. It was a box with some extremely smelly stuff called "Perm."

The scissors worked their magic in Sister's hand as she snipped and snipped. I endured the smelly potent perm as sister poured the solution over my tightly wrapped curls. I had to hide my face in a towel while leaning over the basin. This was to prevent sister from burning my eyes out. Oh, it was some powerful stuff, but it was very necessary to make me beautiful. Just like Shirley.

Sister blew my hair dry and wound my short locks on some metal rollers. I sure felt light headed while looking over at my long golden locks that still lay on the floor. I hoped that sister didn't cut my hair too short. I bet my brothers would think I'm simply beautiful. I hoped.

Sister Carlotta told me to close my eyes as she unwound the rollers from my hair. She wanted the outcome to be a total surprise. I could hardly contain my excitement as sister uttered little words like, "Oh my," and "Goodness." She combed my locks and used a can of hairspray as she sprayed and combed and combed and sprayed. "Come on, Sister," I yelled out loud. "How does it look?" "Do I look like Shirley? Am I beautiful?" After a few more moments I couldn't stand the suspense any longer. I said, Sister you are going to kill me with all the hairspray. I want to see my new self now." Without a word sister handed me the mirror. I stood looking at a hideous image of a girl with frizzy hair. I was shocked and in complete horror.

"That's not me," I yelled. "Oh my God!" I turned to look at sister. "Sister, I'm awful looking! I don't look a thing like Shirley. I'm a big frizz ball! No, I look like a Brillo Pad!" I've never contemplated murder before, but immediately it became foremost in my thoughts.

"I'm kinky and short," I screamed once again as I took one more look into the mirror. "Everyone is going to laugh at me. I'll never be able to go anywhere again. "I just want to die," I screamed. I threw the mirror across the room and pushed at Sister as I ran to make a exit out the door. I mumbled under my breath how unfair and unforgivable this was and I'm sure that Sister was so dumbfounded she didn't know where to turn.

I sat in the corner of my dorm with my hands flung over my head. I don't know how long I sat there. It wasn't long enough. I thought, how could sister do this to me? After a while I felt the tight curls and started sputtering all over again.

Suddenly, the hall bell rang. It was time for dinner. I felt a tremendous rise of panic begin in my chest area. How could I face my brothers and the other children? What would they say? I know that my older brother Jerry loved long flowing hair. Well, he's going to get a good laugh now.

I slowly made my way out of the dormitory and down the stairs to the dining room. I had the weight of the world on my shoulders at the moment and it showed. I made up my mind that I would hate Sister Carlotta for the rest of my life.

As I shyly made my entrance into the dining hall I noticed Sister Carlotta standing at my table next to my brothers. There was a hush that came over the room as I made my grand entrance and I fought wildly to compose myself. I wanted to run and hide and wait until my hair grew back before I saw anyone again, but that would be impossible.

I could plan on Sister Carlotta's murder tonight but looking at her at my dining room table made me realize it really wasn't her fault. So, the only solution left was to face whatever was going to happen and get it over with.

As I approached my assigned table and the one where Sister stood with my brothers, I noticed her hand was extended to give me my glasses. She knew I didn't like anyone to see me without my glasses. That really was thoughtful of her. I pushed the glasses on my nose while making a sly glance in her direction. She placed her hands upon my shoulders and said, "I'm sorry you don't like your haircut. I tried my best." Sister apologized and in front of all the kids.

That took a lot of humble pie on her part. It made me feel somewhat better but still a little sad.

My brother Jerry turned me around to get a good look at me. I looked up defiantly and waited for his comment. "You look pretty, sis," he said. "Not at all like Shirley Temple, but you do look pretty just the same." My brother Bobby chimed in his approval and suddenly my stomach started to growl. I touched my hair again just to assure myself it was still there on my head and gave a smile of complete relief to both of my brothers.

As I entered the serving room, with my tray in hand, several other children nodded their approval. I was starting to feel pretty good about the entire situation. My best friend Barbara said she was going to ask sister to cut and perm her hair just like mine. "I really like it," she said.

As I walked back to the table my thoughts were on Sister Carlotta and how terribly I treated her. I must run upstairs as soon as dinner is over and apologize to her. After all, she did do her best to make my wish come true. Sister didn't make me look like Shirley Temple but she did make me different and as my brother said, "Pretty." I couldn't believe that Barbara wanted a hair cut and perm just like mine. I guess I'm starting my own fad, I said quietly to myself. We can call it the Ruthi Do! I know Sister Carlotta will get a kick out of this I mused. Oh well, I sighed, I didn't die from the whole ordeal and my hair will grow—that's for certain.

A CLOSE CALL

I have been nagged all day by one mysterious thought. Did the Sisters have hair under their habits or were they actually bald? It was time for me to put this question aside and find out the answer. I knew I could find out the answer it was just a matter of when, where and how?

At each different age level, a group of girls would be assigned to one of the Sisters. The ratio would usually work out to be twenty girls to one nun. This sister would then become the surrogate mother to the girls. This process lasted for every two years. Homework, chores, clothing and sleeping assignments all became the duty of that particular Sister in charge. The surrogate Sister had sleeping quarters in the same dormitory with her girls. The quarters consisted of a small area of the dormitory that was enclosed by two walls, a door and a small window. This room was called her cell. The enlacement didn't have a ceiling on it, so Sister could hear what was taking place in the dormitory. Sister could then determine if a child was sick, having a nightmare, or just having a restless evening. It must have been a lonely life for the sisters, and sometimes a heart wrenching chore. For as they listen they could also hear the sobbing that took place every visiting day or the tears of a new child during her first few days of adjustment at the orphanage.

A tremendous idea came to me during supper one evening. I would pretend to have a nightmare! This would force Sister Charlotte, my sister in charge, to come running out of her cell. She wouldn't have time to don her clothing, if timed right. She would want to see what the commotion was all about and then the other girls could see if Sister had hair under her habit. Surely she didn't sleep with that starched habit on her head. What a brilliant idea! It would be so simple.

Evening preparations had begun. I proceeded to tell a few of the girls about my plan. I had to time this nightmare accurately or Sister would see right through the scheme. A rush of excitement started to cruise through my body just imagining the challenge that lay before me.

Sister Charlotte led us in our nightly prayers. After prayers, before we would tuck into our beds, we always recited our little saying in the German tongue. It went like this…"Good night, sweet dreams sleep well and think of me." This was such a simple practice but one I carried on throughout my life. I still remember it today and sometimes I repeat it after my evening prayers.

As I climbed into bed I received several smiles of encouragement from my close buddies. After all, they were excited to see if sister had hair too. The lights were off for what seemed to be an hour…when I started to moan. I didn't want Sister to think I was sick, just having a nightmare, so I let out a yell and then another moan. I tossed and turned and flung my arms to and fro. I shouted some more and even threw-in a few German words. Boy, I was good! I kept my eyes closed for fear of being caught in my endeavor, and soon, I heard Sister Charlotte by my side.

I could tell something was wrong. She didn't turn the dormitory lights on. How could we see her hair without the lights on? I started another moan and quickly flung my eyes open as if awakening from a disturbing sleep. I could see the look of concern in Sister's eyes. I also saw that she had her starched habit on. At first glance, she looked like a mummy that glowed in the dark. The only light in the room came from the top of sister's cell. Of course, looking quickly at her, standing in her habit, put a fear in my eyes. This aided in my plight though. Sister thought I truly had a nightmare. She could plainly see the fear in my eyes. I could have laughed after she retired back to her cell because the only nightmare I suffered from this evening was seeing sister standing next to me in her starched habit, looking like a mummy.

As the following day passed into afternoon, my chance to pursue my thoughts came accidentally. Sister Bernadette said to Sister Robert, "I'll be in the sewing room this evening if you would like a hair cut." That was all I needed to overhear. Now my scheming mind had only to figure out how to see Sister Robert getting this haircut.

The windows of the sewing room overlooked the playground on the boys' section of the home. This made it impossible for us girls to view what was about to happen from the playground. Anyway, the sisters probably closed the shades on the windows to that room. What could I do? There had to be another way. How could I peer into that room? This would take involvement and suggestions from a few of my comrades. We just needed to talk things through.

I challenged Barbara and Bethy to be my accomplices. Both girls were so easy to convince. I really could talk them into anything because they liked a challenge as much as I did. That's what made us such good friends.

Together, we decided the only way to see sister Robert getting a hair cut was to view the incident from the transom window. This was a small window located over the top of the door. It wasn't connected to the door opening but could be opened separately to circulate air to the room. The sisters usually opened the transoms on the doors when a room was being occupied. Hopefully, luck would be with us this particular evening.

Bethy, Barbara and I quietly ran down the long corridor leading to the sewing room. We hoped that no one would see us. The other children were playing on the playground or strolling around the orchard. We had just a half hour to accomplish what we set out to do. Bethy was a dear friend but, like me, she tended to get the giggles whenever she was nervous.

As we passed the chapel, I quickly made the sign of the cross and prayed that we wouldn't get caught in our adventure. Bethy saw me signing and started with the giggles. "Bethy, be quiet. Now is not the time to start laughing," I said. For some reason, fear seemed to grip at my throat and I couldn't giggle even if I felt like it. I did manage to smile at Bethy just to reassure her but I also gave her a stern glance that supported my "no nonsense" warning.

At last we approached the sewing room. The lights were on and we could hear voices and laughter. We heard sister Bernadette say she was ready to cut sister Robert's hair. What luck! We were just in time and, more importantly, the transom was standing wide open.

As usual, a table was standing by the wall of the sewing room. Sister Bernadette used the table to fold and stack items when she completed mending them. One of the children would then take the stack of items and distribute them to the proper places.

Barbara, Bethy and I quietly pushed the table in front of the door. I had to give Bethy a stern look again, warning her not to giggle. I was the first to spring into action as I started climbing onto the table. Standing on tiptoes I peered cautiously in the window. Lo and behold, I couldn't believe what I saw. Sister Robert was sitting in a chair, her habit was removed and she had shiny, dark hair. She looked so different and almost pretty without her habit and veil. What a sight to behold! I motioned for Barbara to climb onto the table to take a look. She couldn't believe what she was viewing either. Not only was Sister Robert sitting without her habit and veil on, she was sitting in her undergarments. She wore a long white slip that exposed her arms. The slip was scooped at the neckline. It was very plain but exquisite in a plain way. Sister Marie and Sister Florence sat in their underwear, too, as they waited their turn for a hair cut.

Bethy wanted to take a look too so we helped her climb onto the table. She took one look at the sisters in their undergarments and without a warning she started to laugh. She tried to stifle her laughter but that only made it worse. Knowing Bethy, it would be impossible for her to stop.

I quickly motioned for her to get down from the table and start running. I turned to warn Barbara but she was yards ahead of us already. Bethy and I ran as fast as we could. We felt as though the sister demons were within inches of us. Soon we caught up with Barbara. The three of us raced down the stairway and out the door that led to the playground. Once we were on the playground we couldn't contain the laughter that had been building up inside of us. We laughed hysterically and clung to one another for several minutes. We couldn't believe that we had succeeded in our adventure. It was unbelievable to pull-off such a stunt. It was unheard of!

Thinking back on the ordeal, it was certainly a good thing that the table was blocking the door when we started to run. It gave us a head start on the Sisters. Trying to visualize the Sisters chasing us in their underwear made us laugh all the harder. What if they were to run into Father Slattery in the hallway! What a sight that would be.

The laughter continued as we lined up with the other girls to go inside for the evening. I kept looking at Sister Charlotte as we stood in line. I wondered what she would look like without her habit and what color would her hair be? I know one thing for certain. I'll never be able to look at any of the other Sisters again without my mind drifting off to my great adventure and close call.

I MADE IT!

Well, I made it into the fifth grade. This is the year that we could join the *choir of angels* if we chose to. But realistically we would have to be selected to join the choir. Have you ever heard the orphan home's choir? It was a mixture of children's voices and a few sisters sprinkled here and there for good measure? It was simply beautiful. Sometimes it was even referred to as celestial.

I could hardly contain my excitement as Monday quickly approached. The day of "the after school choir try-outs," to be held in the chapel promptly at school's end. The entire day in class was torture. I had a hard time keeping silent and sitting still throughout the day.

As the after school bell rang for class dismissal I could feel my stomach churning and my palms start to sweat. Did I really want to do this? Could I even get a note out of my lumpy throat? I started to hyperventilate with all the apprehension.

I somehow made it to the chapel and stood quietly for directives from the main organist, Sister Gilbert. Is she aware that my whole life depends on her judgment in the next 45 minutes? I could hear her reading the names from the sign up list. As she read a name she would then place that person in the proper spot where they were to stand for their judgment. Oh Lordy, she was asking one of the other children to sing,"La La" and "Ohh Ohh's" and to warm up. As my name was called I almost passed out with relief. I was next to the last child to be placed. Could my ears be playing tricks on me? She is placing me right next to herself and the organ. She will hear every note I sing! Every mistake I make!

Sister Gilbert instructed us to stand up straight and take a deep breath. We would begin singing with "Hail Holy King" and later she would divide us into the proper sections for parts.

As Sister Gilbert took her seat and started to play the organ I could feel the silly giggle that was erupting from way deep within my chest. No one has ever told us that Sister Gilbert rotated in a full circle as she played the organ. I kept looking at her with her eyes half closed and circling round. She looked like she was in the midst of a fit! "Oh please don't laugh," I said to myself." Don't even look at anyone, for surely you will loose any semblance of sanity." Oh voice of voices please doesn't fail me now! I started to sing. My voice held a slight tremor in the beginning, but as I closed my eyes and allowed my ears to hear the beauty of the sounds around me, I found a whole new sense of strength that I will never be able to explain to anyone. The louder the organ, the louder and stronger my voice became. My name was second last on the list for sign-ups but at the song's end Sister Gilbert placed my name at the top of the list—of the chosen!

I'll never forget the love, the beauty, and the reverence that overcame me as I took my place next to the organ while Sister Gilbert began to play and sway in her usual fashion. What pride I held in my heart as we sang for every special occasion—always beaming with pride at our celestial harmony.

PICK A NUMBER

While looking through a box of old photographs I came across a picture of three children standing near a bathroom wash basin brushing their teeth. All of a sudden a memory flashed in my mind of the number "29". That was my identification number during those fourteen years in the orphanage.

As I brushed my teeth or combed my hair I could always count on the number 29 being on all the items belonging to me. The sisters painted, sewed and stitched that number on any article as a means of identifying who the item belonged to. This was the practice for each and every child as they passed through the home's doors.

Clothing items were handed down from older children to younger ones. They too had our personal number stitched into the collar. Talking of hand me down clothes reminds me of one of the older girls that was in the home the same time that I was. Her name was Mary Ann. As Mary Ann walked into the chapel she donned a beautiful multi-colored floral dress. The bodice of the dress was trimmed with a tiny red satin ribbon that was complimented by a matching belt of the same shade of red. The dress had a very full skirt and was sleeveless. I thought that this dress was the most beautiful thing I had ever seen. I secretly hoped that in a few years Sister would be sewing my number 29 in that dress.

Mary Ann was a beautiful girl. I believe my brother Jerry had a crush on her. She was very nice to me but sometimes I wondered if she was nice just because of whom my older brother was. It didn't take long and I became a part of the admiration society along with my brother. I wanted to walk and talk just like her. I wanted to have thick brown hair and flashing brown eyes. Whenever she looked my way I was impressed by her beautiful long, dark, eyelashes. She had a way of opening her eyes slowly while sweeping those lashes in a mesmerizing motion. I tried not to let my older brother know how much I admired Mary Ann. I figured he would just make fun of me. I knew that I would never be as pretty or as accepted by everyone as Mary Ann was. I could just dream.

It never failed that as I walked around while imitating Mary Ann, my brother would be watching me and he would then totally freak out on me. I'm sure that if someone gave us a mirror to look at while we both gazed in Mary Ann's direction the reflection would be the same as in my own eyes.

Mary Ann would go out of her way to talk to me on the playground and in the lunchroom. I couldn't understand why she didn't pay attention to me in the laundry room or passing in the dormitory hallways. One thing was for sure, the whole situation backfired when I finally realized that Mary Ann was getting more attention from my brother than I was. She only paid attention to me when my big brother was around. I didn't care for that very much.

It didn't take long for me to figure out Mary Ann's tricks. I was starting to resent her for stealing attention away from me. My time with my brother was very important and I needed for him to pay attention to me. I wanted to scream "phony" to her every time she tried to give me attention when my brother was around. I looked around at other friends and wondered just what they saw in her. Those eye lashes that I once thought were so beautiful were now starting to grate on my nerves. I couldn't believe it but it seemed the more I resented her, the more my brother liked her.

One rainy day in October a new boy came to stay with us in the home. I don't know what number was assigned to him but you could have given him the number "10". He was extremely handsome. He was gifted with broad shoulders and blond curly hair. He had the most beautiful translucent blue eyes that seemed to look right down into a person's soul. And best of all, he was in my older brother's classroom. Mary Ann found his attributes very attractive too as she was seen flashing those famous eyelashes in his direction.

There was no hope for the new boy when Mary Ann turned on the charm.

My brother Jerry was furious. If the new boy did anything—my brother had to do it better. One day Jerry was so mad at the new boy he challenged him to a fight. Before the first swing, Sister Gerald was by his side. She was instructing Jerry to follow her into the classroom where she would teach him how to get along with new people.

Jerry was mortified. He stayed in a gloomy state for a long time.

While in his gloom and doom state he started to watch Mary Ann and noticed how she charmed her way even with the sisters. He said she was like a spider waiting for a fly.

I was saddened by the thought of Jerry being upset. Loosing a girlfriend to such a cool guy wasn't exactly a fun thing. I was glad though that Jerry finally came to his senses. I missed my special time with my big brother and I was so glad—especially when he greeted me with a punch in the arm accompanied by a big "Hi Sis."

THE DISAPPEARANCE TECHNIQUES

It must have been a very difficult job preparing meals for several hundred hungry children. Nevertheless, this was one of the duties that the Sisters performed every day, three times a day, seemingly without effort. I remember how I felt as a child when a certain meal was served that I didn't particularly care for. Actually, my taste buds haven't changed much since my youth, but at least now I have the option not to partake of the foods that aren't appetizing to my palate. Unfortunately, as a child, things weren't quite that easy. My memories went something like this…... "Tonight is the worst night of the month, tonight we are being served liver and onions for supper. Yuck!" I just couldn't muster-up the courage to eat that horrible stuff. Not even if I were starving! The sisters had a way of trying to make us feel guilty when we didn't like a certain food item. It was inevitable that one of the sisters would recite the following little saying whenever a unfavorable meal was prepared to be served.

"There are starving children in China and Africa. You, children, are so very lucky to have this wonderful food to eat. Make sure to eat every bite that is on your plate and remember, be grateful to the Lord, for what you are about to receive!"

Every time I heard that saying…I wanted to scream out loud, "Please sister, give my liver and onions to those poor starving kids. They might even like the stuff!" I truly wouldn't have any problem with giving my portion, gladly. I realized though, that if I ever did utter my thoughts, I would probably wind up picking myself up from the floor! I might have even received a swift kick powerful enough to send me to the unknown lands of China or Africa! Never fear! As children, we had our own way of dealing with the unwanted food situation. We knew exactly how to make food disappear from our plate. The magic of food swapping was taught at a very early age.

One of the ways to "get rid" of a particular food was to make your younger brother or sister eat the delicious morsel. In my case, I was that youngest sibling. Luckily, I liked most foods the sister's prepared so my brother's portions were usually okay by me. They knew, without a doubt, that if I didn't like a particular food, such as liver and onions, it was best not to attempt putting their portion on my plate.

Another way to get rid of food that you didn't like was to swap it with a friend or a neighbor. When you lived with the kids that you ate with, you usually knew who liked what. It was easy to pick-out a friend that you could make exchanges with. There were even certain signals that children would give each other whenever a swap was going to take place. Often, other children assisted in making the swap a success.

Usually, one Sister would supervise in the dining room. This Sister's responsibilities would include keeping order in the dining room while assisting the smaller children with cutting their meat or buttering their bread. We were experts when it came to keeping "sister in charge" busy. It seemed funny that Sister never expressed the fact that on certain days she was kept much busier than on others.

The children all were masters of "the technique of swapping food." It wasn't unusual to see a plate of food sliding across the floor while a swap was in progress. Or you might witness a child raising his or her hand requesting a second helping of food from the serving room. Therefore, the swap would be made while the child was coming from or going to the designated area. Many times a child would simply pick up the food to be swapped and run with it in record time to the awaiting plate of the participating swapper. Thus, another successful exchange was completed!

Swapping food was not only an art confined to the dining room. You see, I was one of approximately fifty children confined to the infirmary with a disease called hepatitis. Some of us were confined up to six months. Sometimes the doctor and the sisters would call us "Yellow Eyes" because the white part of the eye took on a yellow hue. We used to giggle at that name.

During that time we were served daily portions of tapioca. By the fourth month of confinement, I couldn't even look at tapioca much less put it near my mouth.

Since we were watched so closely in the infirmary, it was a real challenge getting rid of the tapioca without Sister noticing. I discovered that if I placed the tapioca into my pajama pocket, which made a real squishy mess, I could then ask to go to the bathroom where immediately I would flush the wiggly mess down the toilet. After flushing I would make sure to rinse my pajama pocket to get rid of any remaining evidence. I was left wearing wet, soggy, pajamas but I didn't mind. It was worth the discomfort just to get rid of the blubbery food.

I would bring my bathrobe with me while heading to the bathroom, thus providing a cover which hid the wet spot from sister's view. Anyway, wearing a bathrobe was the proper thing to do when you were ill.

When I returned from the bathroom I would fake exhaustion. I would crawl under the covers exclaiming the need for a nap. This allowed time for my pajamas to dry while keeping sister from finding out about the tapioca disappearance.

Isn't it funny how, as children, we thought we were so smart and creative. We thought we were really getting away with fooling the Sisters. All the while the sisters were so "into" our little tricks. I'm positive that the Sisters were aware of food exchanges when plates were sliding across the dining room floor. Or maybe they became a little suspicious when a person who never asks for seconds at mealtime would suddenly make a trip to the serving room for seconds by route of a particular friend's table. And I'd bet my bottom dollar that my pajama pockets still contained a trace of sticky tapioca from my duration in the infirmary.

I wish I could have been a little fly buzzing around in the sisters' quarters listening to their tales. I bet that at the end of a hectic day they could tell many humorous stories regarding our little pranks and disappearing tricks. I only hope that the laughter outweighed the hard times. Lord knows, the Sisters certainly deserved a good laugh now and then. I feel positive that we helped somewhat in that respect.

FALL HARVEST TIME

The fall has always been my favorite time of the year. I love the smell of apples cooking over an open fire and burning leaves.

At the orphanage we had a huge apple orchard. After school hours and once homework had been completed, we would change into our play clothes and head outside to the orchard where our gardener, Andy Bogotá, would load us up in the tractor-pulled wagon. We would then be set to go apple picking. There were hundreds of apples everywhere. They were in the trees and on the ground, just waiting for us to grab. My mouth almost waters now, with the thought of scrumptious desserts and "to die for" casseroles that the Sisters would create with all those tasty morsels.

It was a delightful ride in the old wooden wagon. We would laugh and sing while jumping in and out of the wagon. It would never fail that a few of the show-off boys would climb high into one of the trees, just to scare us or watch us hold our breaths and hope they wouldn't have a bad fall. I can't ever remember a single accident occurring during this time.

Andy would pair us up with a friend and give us a wooden basket for our hand picked apples. It didn't take long for the baskets to fill up and old Andy would have to carry the heavy baskets and deposit them into the wagon.

While riding around the home's beautiful grounds, the world just seemed a little brighter and more cheerful. The crisp fall air held a lingering smell of smoke from burning leaves and the sights of the other kids running around the grounds grasping for apples was enjoyable to watch. With the fall time-change evenings got darker fast and much, much cooler. This was my favorite time of year, for sure.

We passed Sister Carlotta as she worked up a sweat raking and stacking leaves into piles. I could see her just puffing away. She really enjoyed this job—at least it seemed that way. Fall must have been her favorite time too. Some of the children were attempting to help her rake but it usually ended up with them spreading her piles of leaves as they jumped in and out of the well packed mounds. I must confess that picking apples was a higher priority to me than raking leaves.

After the apples were collected and the wagon ride was over, a few of the children would help old Andy stack the baskets of apples in the apple cellar. This was located down in the basement of the kitchen. A few of the other children would bring up the big black cooking kettle from the cellar. Now was the time for Sister Bernadette to get out her serious fall recipes. The black kettles were copper lined and would hold at least 25 gallons. I can still smell the wonderful aroma of cooking apples on an open fire. Applesauce has always been one of my favorite dishes.

Sister Bernadette was our head cook and no one questioned her way around the kitchen. She would gather up wooden bowls and arm us girls with paring knives to core and peel the apples. Sister was terrific when it came to the fire and how many logs she wanted the boys to stack under the kettle for her specialties. In the kitchen, Sister Bernadette would prepare apple strudel like none I have ever tasted. She would direct some of the other nuns on the finer points and the proper ingredients for making her famous strudel. The whole time she gave instructions she would fling flour in every direction, all over herself and anyone else that got in her harm's way. The Sisters prided themselves on neatness and cleanliness but during this particular time of the year, I must say, Sister Bernadette did not live up to that description.

After many weeks of coring, peeling and cooking apples, the work would finally be completed. The home was now prepared for a long winter shut-in. Sister Bernadette once again outdid herself by making the most scrumptious treats and yummy desserts. The chores we had accomplished kept us extremely busy but also taught us many things. We learned that being prepared to work hard together would definitely get the job done. And rolling up your sleeves and digging into a job would provide many benefits. Mostly we learned that through teamwork everything could blend in a harmonious joy—the best joy that anyone could expect from a fall harvest.

THE INFATUATIONS

I was in love with a priest. I knew better and I hoped that I wouldn't be damned for my feelings, but oh how I just loved this man. Father Patrick Slattery—now isn't that a strong name? He had black, black hair that was combed straight back from his brow. He had strong intelligent features brought out by beautiful dark brown eyes.

Father was an avid hunter and owned two spirited hunting dogs that were also housed at the orphanage. When we were out on the playground at different times of the day, Father would come out and let the dogs out of their pen for exercise. They would chase us and play with us.

Both dogs were beautiful dogs and were trained to listen to Father's every command. The children were permitted to play with and pet the dogs. But we were warned not to play too rough.

I was one of the first that volunteered to feed, water and brush the dogs. This, of course, allowed me extra time away from the classroom and extra time spent under Father's supervision. Father would compliment me on the good job I did taking care of his dogs. He could in my eyes see the devotion and love that I felt for his dogs, never realizing that the love in my eyes was not for the dogs alone.

Every morning promptly at 6:00 a.m. Mass was said in the chapel. I never missed Mass or my chance to see Father. During Mass I could tell that Father looked at me in a special way. I thought that his gaze was always turned in my direction. Father had special living quarters in the home that were located right down the hall from the chapel . Whenever I was on work-duty in the chapel I kept a special eye on the door where father lived, just to get a glimpse of him as he entered or exited the building, always in a big hurry. This infatuation continued for months until the unforgettable crisis of my life happened.

It seemed that all the girls in the orphan home had either long flowing hair or super short hair. Either way, the sisters liked to curl the girls hair with metal rollers. This would make a very tight, curly hairdo. The metal rollers hurt like the dickens when caught-up in the hair. My hair happened to be extremely long; it hung down to my waist. The nuns used to curl our long hair with rags. This was a two part job. First the rag would be placed over your head and the child would hold one end of the rag. The hair was wound around the part of the rag that sister held in her hand. Lastly, the part of the rag that the child held was then wound on top of the hair and a knot would tie the ends together, keeping the entire curl together. This process would take at least 12 to 15 rags per child depending on the thickness of the hair. When the rags were removed the result would be beautiful, dangling banana curls.

One particular Saturday, Sister Paul had just completed my rag curls. I had a total of 15 rag curls and knots. Sister Lacertian from the laundry room needed some help with the backed up laundry and since I was on laundry room duty during this week, I had to report to Sister Lacertian for duty. It was a chilly November Saturday, one of those days that when the wind blew it created a howling sound.

I put my coat on and my scarf around my neck and headed out the door to the laundry room, which was located in a different building behind the home. The last words I heard from Sister Paul as I ran out the door was to put the hood up on my coat up to cover my newly curled and still damp hair.

Once out the door, I started to run; I was trying to keep the wind from my face and hoping to shorten my trip. My hood flew off of my head and my scarf was whipping around my throat. There simply wasn't time enough to place my hood back on my head or try to secure my scarf around my neck. Anyway I almost reached my destination. All of the sudden out of the corner of my eye I could see something flashing white.

Never would I have guessed in a million years that Father Slattery was out walking his hunting dogs. I couldn't believe it, not now, I just couldn't run into Father Slattery looking like this! My thoughts screamed inside my head. Surely he will laugh out loud at me.

Well, the two hunting dogs didn't seem to care about my dilemma. They didn't care that I was the person who fed and watered them for weeks. They only saw the rags and knots in my hair and I sure must have looked like a real hunting prize to them. The next thing I knew, I was down on the ground with two dogs gnawing and pulling at the rags in my hair. My scarf was so tight around my neck I could hardly scream and my dress was positioned in the most un-lady like fashion. What a sight I must have made. If a person could just fade into the concrete on command then that would have been my desire. I firmly believed that I was in death's waiting arms. Soon, I would become lunch to two hungry, gnawing dogs. Nevermore would I be able to look into the eyes of my beloved Father Slattery.

Huge hands started to lift me from the ground and a strong, verbal command was given to the growling dogs. In no time at all I was standing with rags about my feet and Father Slattery was trying to un-wrap my scarf from about my neck. How humiliating! How horrid! How demeaning! My tears were uncontrollable as Sister Lacertian came running from the laundry room. She must have seen the whole episode from her window. She was scolding Father Slattery's dogs while trying to soothe my hurt and injured pride.

Once seeing that I was going to live, Father Slattery turned to leave with his dogs. I walked to the laundry room where I managed to put myself back in order with a little help from Sister. Nothing would ever be the same again. I could never look Father Slattery in the face, nor could I ever feed or take care of his dogs.

The next morning at Mass, I knew that Father Slattery kept looking my way. I couldn't look up at him. I'd never be able to do that again. Feeling humiliated, I looked at my friend Barbara instead. Wow, Barbara was looking at father with such goggle eyes.

I must say she was almost drooling. I had to ask myself if I used to look at Father in the same way. Did I look that helpless and silly? I turned to look at Father once more when suddenly; all I could do was smile. The entire situation became quite funny. How silly I have been. He is a wonderful person and has been a true friend. He has always shown concern for all of us children and we all loved him in our own special way. It was wonderful to realize that I wasn't in love with Father Slattery but loved him. I couldn't help the sense of loss that rose from deep within me. It almost seemed like a relief!

Thinking about the scene I must have created, made me start to giggle. Once again I cast a glanced at Father Slattery only to see that he was watching me with a smile on his face too. We shared an experience that neither one of us would ever be able to forget. We would always have this special something to remember and chuckle about.

I slowly turned to leave the chapel. A smile was still playing across my lips. Without thinking and completely absorbed in my own train of thought, I ran smack into the chest of one of the boys. He had a scowl on his face as his eyes pierced into mine. Abruptly I stopped thinking about Father Slattery and our little episode. There was something in the look that Donald was giving me. He knew how I felt about Father Slattery. I don't know how—but he knew.

Before I could understand my feelings, my thoughts no longer were consumed by a Priest. I truly liked the way Donald kept looking at me as I made my way slowly out the chapel doors right past the living quarters of Father Slattery. A warm feeling started to churn its way into my heart as a mysterious smile claimed my face. An image and name of a very special boy with amber colored eyes popped hauntingly into my head. My mind was whirling with scenes from our special meeting.

NO MORE CHALLENGES

Chewing gum was one pastime that was forbidden in the home. I could probably count on one hand the amount of gum I've chewed by the time I was fourteen years old. Now candy, that was different since candy was a luxury. Candy was only given to the children on very special occasions and then, in very small quantities. Thus, the older I became, the bigger my sweet tooth developed.

I'm not sure if the sisters really knew what my friends and I were up to this balmy day in June, but rest assured, we were up to something. If the sisters even had a clue to what we were about to do they would have tied us to a chair or locked us in our dorm room and then dispose of the key.

The children spent a lot of time with benefactors and guests while they were visiting the orphanage. Special times like the home's picnics took place twice a summer and the children would have a lot of time interacting with the benefactors of the home. It was very easy to talk with these special people. This was our special chance to let them know just how hard it was to go through life without little luxuries like gum and candy. They would share packs of gum with us in all sorts of flavors. One would be amazed at the squeals of excitement when a visitor would pull out an assorted bag of candy for the children to share. Soon, visitors would be listening to hints or appeals from the children regarding items they could bring on their next visit to the home. This became a game for all of the children, from the youngest to the oldest. We learned very quickly.

It wasn't long before we started receiving money along with the gum and candy. We really didn't have any use for money, growing up the way we did, but it sure was fun receiving so much attention.

Several of the girls were discussing the idea of taking a pack of cigarettes. I never would have thought of doing such a thing on my own but we did have a couple of girls that lived on the outside of the home for a number of years. I guess being quizical about cigarettes would have been a normal thing for kids our age—I don't know. I do know that I never cared for the way cigarettes smelled and so I just didn't think of trying to smoke one. Well, the stage had been set by one of the older girls. She looked in my direction and a dare came around my way without even a chance for me to prepare a denial. Immediately, I had to accept and my thoughts turned toward the perfect little gentleman who could help me get through still another challenge.

This sweet old gentleman had to be at least 104 years old. His hair was completely white and he had false teeth that made a clicking sound whenever he spoke. He loved to indulge in the "drinking of German beer." He would become the perfect target for my perfect crime.

You could pick him out in any crowd because he was the one person that had a halo of smoke following him everywhere. He liked to smoke. He usually didn't put his cigarettes back in his pocket, after he lit one up. He would leave them laying on the table right next to where he sat. This made it easy for him to light up the next one before he was finished with the one he was currently puffing on. Well, this should make my task quite easy.

With this ultimate dare in mind I put my plan into action. As my cigarette friend liked to drink, I told him I would save his seat and watch his cigarettes if he wanted to fill his cups again. I felt a little tinge of guilt knowing I was taking something from this trusting, kind old gentleman but the dare was more prevalent at this moment than my feelings of mistrust. I reached for the cigarettes and matches as soon as my gentleman made his way to the beer wagon. I only took a couple of cigarettes and then ran as fast as I could toward the safety of my dormitory.

My face shone bright red as guilt consumed me. Anyone who knew me could tell that I had just committed a huge sin. All anyone would have to do was look into my eyes for as Sister Paul often stated, "my eyes told all."

None of the girls involved in this dare were going to believe that I actually succeeded and it was so simple.

My best friend Barbara was running down the stairs as I was running up them. Immediately I motioned that I had succeeded in getting our little package. We just needed a place to meet the other girls and it would have to be soon. I certainly didn't want to be caught with this contraband.

Shortly, Debbie grabbed my arm and asked if I succeeded in my mission. Of course every time she approached me on any subject it had to be with an audience present. It was very hard to like Debbie. I believe that in this day and age Debbie would be tagged with the name "control freak." I haughtily tossed my head in the direction of the hidden cargo and began to brag on how easy it was to succeed with the challenge. I explained every cunning detail of how I boldly slipped several of the cigarettes from the pack into my dress pocket and made my exit. "Easy as pie," I explained. Debbie couldn't believe that "miss goody two shoes," as she so lovingly called me, could get away with such a dare. I looked into her eyes and I could tell she was not celebrating in my success. She pretended she was impressed but she was always good with pretense. While looking at her, another moment came into my mind's view, of Debbie's first day in the orphanage.

She came to us very late in life. She must have been around ten years old. I remember her crying for days and days. She did not want to be in the orphanage. She wanted to go back home with her family.

Debbie cried so hard for so many days she actually rubbed scabs and sores on her cheeks. My heart broke for her, but I just couldn't understand why anyone would hate the home that much. I loved this place and in time I knew she would learn to love it too. I found out through Sister Florence that Debbie had lost both parents in a fire. She didn't have any other brothers or sisters. She did have one aunt who lived out of town. She was going to stay with us in the home until other arrangements could be made for her.

It was hard to think that Debbie had such a loving family and then in one day's time it was all gone. She truly was an orphan in the home.

My attention was brought immediately back into focus when I heard the words, "well, since no one is around, this would be the perfect time to sneak up to the attic and smoke a cigarette." I couldn't believe I was hearing this. For one thing, the attic was not a place that you would want to visit. It was forbidden for any of us children to go there without one of the nuns in attendance. It was very dark, very scary and very, very big. What in the world were we thinking of? After mumbling something incoherently I was jerked back to reality by the look on Debbie's face. She had a devilish grin from ear to ear and she was staring right at me. I just knew that she was somehow related to the EVIL one.

I grabbed the cigarettes from my pocket and handed them to Debbie. If we were going to chance walking the halls then she could carry the incriminating evidence. We climbed the steps by twos. Our hearts were racing in competition with our running legs.

It was an almost exhilarating feeling when we opened the door to the attic and hurriedly closed the big door behind us. We made it to the top floor without anyone seeing us. None of the Sisters were around, with the picnic going on. The Sisters would be too busy with seeing to all the arrangements and duties that had to be done that day.

As we looked around the attic we came to the total agreement that it didn't look so bad during the daytime. There were many windows on all sides of the attic so this really helped to lessen our fears. The heat was horrendous though. I thought of opening a window but couldn't take the chance that someone would see it and give us away. We looked around the attic and just couldn't believe all the boxes of things that were stored there.

I sat remembering the times we would help Sister Gilbert bring our Halloween costumes up here in the attic for storage. We would dress up on Halloween in many different fabrics and scarves. We celebrated the eve of all Saints Day. There were miles and miles of fabric used to play dress up along with colored belts and shiny shoes.

We were to dress like and represent our Patron Saint on this day. After getting dressed up we would parade all around the home and the sisters would have to guess who we were and what saint we represented.

After that we would all go to the auditorium and have a small party, including apples and oranges for treats. The evening would usually end with a hand selected movie and tasty popcorn. The sisters usually let us stay up past 9:30 on that particular evening. We really thought we had it made and we did!

Debbie was asking me if I brought any matches with me or did I manage to take Mr. Patrowski's lighter? Boy, she was really getting on my last nerve! I stated that the cigarettes were all that was required of my dare and it wasn't in my plan to take anything else. Debbie just looked at me and smiled. She opened her hand and right in the center of her palm laid a book of matches. I didn't feel relieved at the sight of the matches. I had a horrible feeling about this whole incident and if it wasn't for "Little Miss Debbie" I would have been out of there in a second.

Debbie lit the first cigarette and handed it to me. I passed it on to Barbara with a shrug. Barbara took the first puff and handed the cigarette back to me. I passed it on to Debbie and smiled. She took a puff and handed it back to me with a smile. I was doomed. I didn't even know how to do this. Of course my palms were sweaty and my lips were dry. I put the cigarette to my lips and inhaled. I tried to pull the cigarette away from my lips because I had a horrible urge to cough and gag. The cigarette stuck to my dry lips and I burned my fingers. I thought I would tear the skin off my lips as I removed the cigarette from my dry lips so I could put my burned fingers in my mouth. They hurt so badly. I was so preoccupied with my dilemma that I didn't notice Barbara and Debbie coughing and moaning. Debbie was insistent that she would become an accomplished cigarette smoker so she tried again and again.

She puffed and coughed then started again. She conned Barbara into puffing more and more and suddenly right before my eyes both girls turned a deathly pale green. Both were moaning and sweating profusely. Barbara became extremely sick. The heat of the attic wasn't helping at all. I ran over to one of the side windows and opened it for fresh air.

As I peered out the window gulping in the fresh air I saw sister Carlotta looking up at the open attic window. Oh drat! Of all the windows I picked to open I had to pick the one that old eagle eyes would be attracted to. There was no doubt in my mind that she saw me hanging out the window. Our fate had been sealed.

I ran back to Barbara and Debbie and explained our situation. Neither girl cared if Sister Carlotta saw me or not. They both just wanted to be left alone to die. I quickly closed the window and hid the cigarette and matches in one of the boxes close to the window that had Father Slattery's name on it. Surely this would be a safe place. Then I was faced with the dilemma of getting Debbie and Barbra down the stairs and back to the dormitory before Sister Carlotta made an appearance.

Sister Carlotta never showed up in the dormitory and Sister Paul was in the process of coaxing some type of potion down Debbie and Barbara's throats. She felt sorry for the two of them since they evidently ate something very bad at the picnic. She couldn't believe how sick the two girls were. Why, they almost looked green to her! It could have been a comic situation, both girls trying to drink Sister Paul's concoction and feeling as sick as they were. But my fears were still at hand and I couldn't think of laughing at any situation. Sister Carlotta saw me at the window. I just knew it! She was looking up at the window. I agonized at the thought of seeing Sister Carlotta at any moment.

My thoughts turned to Debbie once again. How utterly stupid I was to allow myself to be challenged to such a dumb dare. Debbie was getting her just dessert right now. I felt sorry for Barbara though. She was such a true friend. I could con her into anything.

Time for kitchen duty drew near. We still had our chores to do no matter what the celebration was, picnic day or not. I showed up a few minutes early for duty and guess who I was assigned to. Sister Carlotta's back was facing me. I knew her back anywhere. Oh Lord, I still had time to run or face my demise. I decided enough was enough. I would take what was coming and get it over with. Sister Carlotta looked at me in her usual stern way and slowly her eyebrow raised and she said.

"Are you going to stand there staring all day or what? Let's get to work."

She didn't see me! She didn't know!" Oh infant Jesus, you did help me out. I grabbed an apron and started washing the pile of pots and pans that were stacked on the cart near the sink. Sister Carlotta must have thought I was completely out of my mind as I smiled and started to wash. She had never seen me so excited to do dishes. Usually I complained about my dishpan hands just to hear Sister moan.

I felt the most excruciating pain as I placed my burnt fingers in the water. Sister Carlotta looked my way and suddenly she held a soft expression as she questioned what happened to my lip. There seemed to be a sore on my lip. What happened? I told her that I had a little accident while running up the steps. Oh I hate lying to her that way. I made a vow on that very spot that I would never let myself get involved with any more of Debbie's challenges. It simply wasn't worth it.

As I looked into the dish water a smile crossed my lips, for once again my thoughts returned to my two friends in the dormitory suffering not only from the cigarette adventure but from this horrible concoction they had to endure.

Just as quickly, reality struck once again and my thoughts were about another problem at hand. If those two so called friends of mine were sick then just who was going to take their turn working in the kitchen? Who alone was going to keep scrubbing all the pots and pans? The answer was obvious. The challenge was mine alone.

COMPLEXITIES OF THIRD GRADE

It was a beautiful spring day. The sun was filtering through the window, casting a blinding glow on my desktop. I closed my eyes letting the sun fall across my face. It felt warm and toasty. I glanced out of the window, wanting to be anywhere but in the classroom. I loved this time of year. I could see a mound of colorful flowers hovering around the statue of St. Vincent. Just a few weeks ago the view from this window was so very different. I listened a little more intently and could hear the roar of the tractor as Mr. Bogotá, our grounds man, cut the grass.

I thought to myself, "what a terrible time to be stuck in a classroom."

This was the final week of third grade. We were all very antsy to be out of school and greet the ever-wonderful summer!

Sister Florence was my third grade teacher. I remembered waiting for what seemed to be a lifetime to have her for a teacher. My brother Bobby would tell me stories about his favorite teacher, Sister Florence. She would give the class candy during school hours and was considered "easy" when it came to giving grades. He spoke so highly of this nun and of her "smiling ways."

Well, I definitely was going to give my brother a piece of my mind. During this entire year of school not one student has seen a single piece of candy. And as far as "easy" grades go! Whew! There hasn't been an easy grade given yet. Sister didn't have a good side to get on. Maybe she just liked the boys better and was easier on them.

I must say though, Sister Florence was a terrific painter. We loved to see her draw and paint. Somehow everything always came out beautiful. Since art was among my favorite things to do, and something that I did well....my attention crawled reluctantly back into the classroom, leaving Mr. Bogotá to continue cutting the grass on his own.

With paint brush in hand, I turned my total concentration on the assignment before me. We were in the process of learning how to draw and paint beautiful dogwood flowers on a greeting card. In the center of the card was a square that we would carefully cut out. Our school photograph would then be inserted into this spot, completing a beautiful "work of art." Sister Florence would say in her high pitched voice, "the art will then be a reflection of you!"

I had a tendency to get real excited while doing something that I truly enjoyed. And at that particular moment it was hard to contain my excitement. I never realized before, but my mouth gets to chattering 100% of the time when I get excited. I'm also sure that this talking has to be linked to some type of a disorder. I don't know what the name of this disorder is although I'm sure my doctor would be able to identify it, if I had one. A doctor, I mean. He could label it as something called "jabber-al-ity" or "talk-ing-ite-ess" or "speak-eez-en-ly?" I'm quite sure that one of those names would be an appropriate term for the disorder. You do know what I'm talking about, don't you?

Each stroke of the brush brought out another and still another sound from my mouth. Emphatically and I might add very loudly, Sister Florence stated, "Enough!"

"If you cannot create a piece of art without your mouth continually going then we will have to find a solution for your problem," she further stated. Well, I knew to whom that little speech was directed.

Try as hard as I might, I could not contain myself. Sister Florence quietly approached me. She placed her hands on mine to still my brush strokes. As I peered into her eyes, I knew without a hesitation that a solution was at hand. Sister Florence pulled a roll of masking tape from deep within her apron pocket. Skillfully she proceeded to tape my mouth closed.

The other children in the classroom were in complete awe as Sister skillfully completed her task. She handed me back my paint bush and motioned for me to continue with my project in silence. I started dipping the brush in the gentle pink paint. As I stroked the brush across the paper a smile appeared clearly in my eyes as I defiantly hummed a cheerful little tune.

Sister Florence expelled a deep sigh as she dramatically but pointedly walked over to the classroom supply cabinet. Out of the cabinet she pulled a stash of luscious, assorted candies. Then she began smiling and humming her own little tune as she swayed from aisle to aisle placing tiny morsels on the other students desks. Periodically, she gave a glance in my direction as she charmed all the other children in the class with samples of her tasty goodies. It didn't take long for me to stop humming. My mouth watered for the tempting goodies that everyone else was enjoying.

As I continued with my art project, in silence, I began to add up the growing list of things I needed desperately to discuss with my older brother. Mainly, we needed to discuss the complexities of his very favorite third grade teacher.

A SPECIAL BIG BROTHER

My brothers and I sat quietly in the large waiting room that was designated for special visits, such as this one we were anticipating from our family counselor. We listened intently for the whimsical chime of the door bell proclaiming that our visitor had arrived.

Ms. Berma Pape, our counselor, made her presence known by entering the room like a whirlwind. She had just climbed the large flight of stairs, entering the lobby of the orphanage, with bags clung tightly in each of her hands and wearing one of the silliest drooping hats I had ever seen. Her glasses were positioned low on the bridge of her nose and she spoke with a very thick German accent! A strong smell of garlic permeated the air, apparently the remains from her "lunch on the go."

An old mahogany grandfather clock stood in the corner of the parlor ticking away the minutes until our meeting would start. On the other wall of the room was a beautiful painting of the Guardian Angel. The angel was standing behind two very small children. Her arms were wrapped around the children in a protective manner. I often pictured myself as one of those small children in the protective custody of such a loving defender.

Sister Boniface worked for years as the home's secretary. She was a short, rotund little nun with a perfectly round face matching her round figure. Everyone knew she wasn't used to being around the children. She would get so nervous when a child was around that her face would redden and I do believe she broke out in a rash. Paper work, files and phone communication were her specialty and she excelled in them.

Sister Boniface instructed the three of us children to sit quietly, mind our manners and think before we answered any questions that Ms. Pape would ask. I noticed that Ms. Pape carried several bags in her hands as she came into the room. I assumed Ms. Pape knew more about us children and our background than we could ever imagine and our entire life history was in those three bags.

Truth be known, Ms. Pape was a kind old maid that honestly loved children. I'll never understand why she tried to appear so gruff and tough. No one could deny her dedication as a social worker with the long hours, low pay and helplessness that became her constant companions visit after visit. I guess her only satisfaction came from the successful results she received from a few of her families.

Visits from Ms. Pape were harmless. Sometimes they were even humorous. She asked how we were, and if we needed anything. She asked if we had any questions or were wondering about anything. Most of the time, we didn't have any questions. As children what could we ask? Or what could we need? We never did understand the purpose for the visits. We did resent the fact that the visits almost always happened during our play time instead of class time.

During this particular visit, for some unknown reason, I paid attention to a comment that Ms. Pape made while talking to Sister Boniface. The comment referred to our poor "sick" mother and then our "absent" father. Curiosity almost killed me. You see, I understood that we had a mother that was very sick and couldn't ever take care of us, but no one ever mentioned our father. I assumed that everyone has a father; ours was just missing...somewhere.

I asked very quietly and emphatically and I thought before I spoke, which was very unusual for me. My question was "where is our father?" With that question out in the open Sister Boniface's grew a shade redder, if that were possible. She was determined to make a quick exit.

She mumbled something about typing that needed her attention immediately. Ms. Pape started to stutter as if I were the one speaking in a foreign tongue. Suddenly, she put her files on the table and began to answer my question." You see children," she began. "You do have a father. However, he lives very far away in a place called Rhode Island. He is presently married to a wonderful lady and they have a family of their own. When your father was contacted by my office regarding his duties as a father to the three of you...well, he expressed that he didn't want his present family to know anything about his past or about his other children. He wanted a new beginning and a life of his own. He requested not to be contacted again."

I just sat there trying to absorb what I had just heard. I could see tears in my brother Bobby's eyes. Jerry said nothing but I could tell that wasn't a good thing. Quickly I spoke out to break the silence. "Well, if he doesn't want me to be a part of his family then I don't want him either." I couldn't say too much more because my insides felt as though they were about to crumble. All kinds of thoughts started to enter my mind. I didn't even know what he even looked like—so, I asked.

"He has very dark red hair and very blue eyes," was Ms. Pape's reply. "Well, I really don't care," I shouted. "I guess he must look like Bobby then,? Bobby has red hair and light blue eyes I stated." Was he tall or short?" The reply was tall. "Will he ever come to see us?" was the next question. But as soon as those words were out of my mouth I wished I could grab them back. "I don't think your father will visit you anytime soon children," Ms. Pape replied in a whisper. I swore I could see tears in her eyes.

I didn't have any more questions so I asked to be excused in a faint voice. I didn't wait for a reply. I had to make an escape from the truth. It hurt too much. I hugged my brothers and with my small hands clinging to the insides of my pockets I left the room. I didn't want to think or feel ever again. I sat quietly in the chapel. Tears threatened to spill from my eyes. I pondered over the session with our social worker. At least I knew that somewhere out there I had a father. I knew that someday he would come for my brothers and me. He had to. If he would just visit us once—I know he would want us. We really are good and we wouldn't be a problem to him ever or his new family.

While thinking of the qualities that make up a father, the only person that came close to mind was my oldest brother Jerry. Jerry protected me when other children were cruel. He taught me my table manners and how to spread my bread. Often as a child I would slip into a babyfied speech, mostly for a little attention. It was Jerry who understood me and would make me talk like a little lady instead. When I was sick and confined to the infirmary—it was my big brother Jerry, whom would visit me, even without permission from the sisters. He made me smile when I had swollen glands and it hurt like the dickens. He would always give me a special wink when I passed him in the hallway or a special squeeze of the hand whenever I was feeling alone. He was not only my big brother but a father image to me. He saved me from the terrible ache of needing a father. He was big, called the shots and I loved him.

I could never explain how hard it was the day my older brother left the orphanage. I was so proud of him as he graduated. He would be starting a new life, a new beginning without Bobby and me. Oh how I would miss him! My heart was pounding in my throat. I felt as though I was going to choke. After Jerry left I walked in a stupor while tears seeped from my eyes for weeks. During meals my brother Bobby and I sat staring at the empty chair where our big brother once sat. Jerry never forgot us though. He came back for Sunday visits. Finally, Bobby and I had someone to visit us on these special days. It became our special ritual for a while, every second Sunday of the month you could find us visiting with our big brother. That lasted until Jerry decided to enter the Army. He was only 17 years old at that time. Little did he know that a whole new life was waiting for him? It might sound strange to some, but when Father's Day rolls around, I take a few moments of the day thinking about my fond memories of my older brother. He is the one that taught me, in his own special way, the patience and devotion of a father's love.

PRIDE IN COMPETITION

It was winter and Christmas was behind us. We were experiencing a bleak and dismal January. The cold outside condensed the warmth from the radiators and left the windows wet and fogged. Just perfect for printing one's name or the name of the handsome boy that filled your daily dreams. Alone and standing next to one of those densely fogged windows, I couldn't resist putting the tip of my finger to the cold glass and very lethargically start to write the forbidden name of my dreams.

It was time for any interested kids to volunteer for the upcoming skating show competition. We had a very nice roller skating rink in the orphanage located just below the gym. I loved to skate. This was one thing I could excel in. I've been noted to have muscular legs and this sure was a benefit when skating.

The theme for this year's skating show, held at Hodges Skating Rink, was "Germany." How fortunate for us that half of our nuns were from Germany and spoke in the German tongue. This surely was a good omen.

The members of the Hodges Skating Rink made the scenery and props. They included snowcapped mountains, Austrian pine trees, houses donned with gingerbread decorations, and a small town that boasted a huge town hall loaded with German beer steins. Beer barrel props would be grouped together in threes for jumping and an actual slope was created for a skiing appearance. Instructions for the skating performance were given to each group of competitors. Costumes were to be made by the competitors also. The skating routines had to include a series of jumps, slides, partner as well as individual routines. The rest was up to the skaters and their coaches to pull the whole program together.

Practice was a farce. Kids fell on top of each other while goofing around. Pairs refused to hold hands with one another while doing their routine, barrel jumper's skated alongside of the barrels instead of completing their jumps...no one seemed to take the program seriously. Sister Gilbert was the person responsible for choreographing the entire project. She was surely in the running for "sainthood." Sister repeatedly stopped the music just as it seemed to get started, making it difficult for the pairs to understand their routine or get their rhythm down pat. Organ music never was my favorite type of music but it did seem to compliment skating.

I'll never forget a particular scene, as Donald James, who was my boyfriend in those days, tried to make the three barrel jump. Donald tried and tried to complete the jump. Often, he landed sideways, or did a complete belly flop landing on top of the barrels. The more Donald tried the harder the task became and the more bullheaded he became. I'm sure glad that we didn't practice at Hodges Rink before the show. The whole world would have looked at us as complete fools. Sister Paul, the patient one, would sit at the sewing machine for hours sewing her magic. It was amazing to see the costumes she created with her crafty skills. I know this sounds silly, but once the children put those costumes on they started skating like professionals.

Practice continued on a nightly basis. I remember one evening in February when the entire program almost seemed to go flawlessly until the barrel jump came. Donald seemed hesitant. I was skating with three other girls. It was our skating routine to be on the opposite side of the room as Donald made his triple jump. The four of us would lock left hands in the air, while the right hand held the bottom of our roller skate with our leg outstretched, parallel to our heads.

I watched Donald as he approached the barrels and I could tell by watching that he just wasn't going complete the jump. My hands started to clam up as a cold sweat beaded my brow. The three girls and I were in perfect unison on the opposite side of the rink. Our legs extended high in the air while skating at full speed. I couldn't take my eyes off Donald. I didn't see that the girl on the outside of our line had skidded on a ball bearing from someone's skate. She gracefully landed on the floor pulling the girl next to her on the floor too. I didn't want a turn on the floor, so I immediately let go of my partner's hand. I glanced once more to see if Donald made his jump and he had...it was perfect!

Still with a slight smile on my face after witnessing Donald's successful jump, I turned to see a blurred green stripe rushing toward me. At the speed I was skating it was impossible to come to a stop—not to mention I was completely frozen. I'm sure I left an impression on the other skaters as I still clung to my skate in the air while slamming into the wall.

I landed in the infirmary for two weeks. I had severely pulled every ligament in my legs. I knocked myself out, bruised every part of my body, and the doctor proclaimed no more skating. I never realized that even your hair could hurt.

Well, I was given permission with strict orders from the doctor that if I would sit quietly and not get too excited, I could go to the skating rink and watch the skating show in its entirety. No one would be able to guess how proud I was of my orphan home family. Sister Paul far exceeded her sewing ability. The girls' dresses were simply breathtaking. They were of bright red with rickrack lining the hem. A black cover was placed over their skates adorned in different sequin colors. The boys wore the traditional German shorts and their heads donned the Austrian hat with different colored plumes. Their skating was breathtaking as they glided and swayed to the music.

The time approached for Donald to do his three barrel jump and the girls to skate in unison with legs in the air. My breath and heart stopped for the few moments—completion!! All was perfect. The girls, just the three had impeccable timing and Donald—well he stole the show. Everyone at the rink was standing and clapping in unison. Needless to say, the competition was a shoe-in.

As I would hurry to my classroom on the third floor of the home, I would often take a few minutes to run downstairs and grab a quick peek at the roller skating trophy in the gymnasium trophy case. Even though I didn't participate in the competition, I feel I was a big part of the team. The pride I felt that wintry day while watching my team skate will remain locked in the heart of my memories forever.

A SECRET WEEKEND

It still mattered to me that all the kids had gone home for the week-end. My older brothers had been gone from the home for several years now. I was the last one in my family still remaining. I hated days like this when everyone was gone for the holidays. Echoes of greetings still could be heard in the distant hall. This always left me missing my brothers terribly. I especially missed the times we shared discussing our daily activities over the dinner table. It bothered me that I didn't realize how important those times were until both brothers had left.

I helped several of my friends pack their suitcases for their week-end visit. It was getting harder to hug them goodbye and tell them to have a wonderful visit. I wanted to pack myself in their suitcases and get away too! I was very sincere when I expressed my wishes for them to have a fun-filled visit and to enjoy their family time together. It was always afterwards, when I waved goodbye and watched until their car coasted down the street and out of my view, that the ever present tears would sting my eyes and my heart threatened to break into tiny pieces. Oh, how I wished I had someone who wanted to share their time and their dreams with me! Holidays were supposed to be fun and special. Holidays were supposed to be family and love. Holidays shouldn't mean sadness and loneliness.

I was the only girl left in the dormitory who didn't have a special place to go. I found myself meandering from room to room actually wallowing in self-pity. I missed the sounds and activities of my friends in the dorm. I missed having someone to laugh with or bicker back and forth with.

Sister Paul was worried about me and she asked if I was all right. I told her not to worry. I guess my words said one thing but my face showed another. She did worry about me though and I knew it. When I thought about it, Sister Paul wasn't going any place either. None of the sisters were. They were stuck here with me! I'm sure at times they felt lonely too! I don't know why I never realized that before!

It was Easter break and spring was early this year. The warm sun beating upon my upturned face felt wonderful. The sun always had a healing effect on my soul. I could sit here all day against this sturdy apple tree, breathing in the perfumed fragrance that permeated the air from the newly open blossoms.

I sat alone for a while dreaming of a perfect white house with huge paned windows. The windows were framed with emerald green shutters. A tiny white kitten was perched in one of the upstairs windows. He sat looking out lazily upon a manicured lawn filled with flowers of every texture and color imaginable.

A blazing red car pulled up in front of my dream house and a laughing girl with hair, my exact color, bounced out of the back seat holding onto a suitcase. She yelled her greetings to the purring creature in the window as she ran head-on to the outstretched arms of her mother waiting on the sunlit porch. I could almost smell the perfume her mother was wearing. The girl reached up to give her mother a hug. As her mother bent slowly to receive her child's love, her soft velvety hair tickled the girls nose. My nostrils itched with this vision, causing me to sneeze.

The sun was hiding behind a billowy cloud and the air became cooler as my dream faded with the warmth of the day. The old tree seemed to scratch into my back and my outstretched legs tingled from lack of circulation.

It was time for me to head back to the dorm and see what Sister Paul was up to. Sister Paul was hunched over her sewing machine, preoccupied with one of the dresses she was mending. The radio blasted an old Elvis tune as Sister's sewing machine seemed to keep time to the tune of "Blue Hawaii."

I didn't know that Sister Paul listened to the radio when the children were gone! It never occurred to me that silence was not to her liking either. I guess with the children gone, Sister Paul was at a loss for what to do with her time.

I stood watching as Sister began to hum the song with Elvis. Suddenly she broke out singing the words with her usual clear voice. I stepped back to assess the situation around me. Sister was a small boned lady and not very tall at all. Her eyes were a soft brown and clear as a doe's skin. If I had to say so myself, Sister Paul was quite beautiful. I suddenly had the urge to run up behind her and give her a bear hug. What would she do? Lord knows, my arms ached to hug someone. Would she care?

Sister Paul turned in her chair and met my gaze. How did she know I was standing behind her? She smiled at me and her entire face seemed illuminated. "You know kiddo; I sure could use a hug about now, how about you?" I couldn't believe that sister had heard my thoughts. I flung myself into her waiting arms.

I hugged her with every force in my being. She in turn, hugged me back with the same intensity. We didn't hurry. Time wasn't relevant. The tears that were present all day had succeeded once again to claim my soul. Sister soothed my face and my heart in her knowing manner. She spoke in a gentle voice letting me know that I would be all right. I was a survivor like her and she knew my heart would mend.

All too abruptly, Sister stood from her chair and, with a gleam in her eye she challenged me to a monopoly game. Well, master of the game that I was, the challenge was accepted wholeheartedly.

Sister and I played the game for hours. We laughed, we shouted loudly as we cheered each other on——we enjoyed!

It was past 9:00 o'clock in the evening. I couldn't believe I was still up at this time of the night. Sister Paul and I were sitting in the dorm joined by several other sisters. We were watching television and I was clad only in my pajamas. We children were never allowed to watch television this late into the evening. I certainly felt like I was enjoying a part in a forbidden play.

I glanced over at Sister Bernadette as she strolled into the dorm with bowls of popcorn for us to share. I couldn't stop looking around at the Sisters as they chatted and ate and watched the television. They certainly deserved a rest from the children and their daily responsibilities. I was in shock to see how they really enjoyed themselves. I only wished my friends could see the Sisters as I did at this moment. Sister Florence sat with her feet planted up on a table (which was forbidden). Sister Robert talked while chewing on her popcorn at the same time. (Can you believe it?) Sister Carlotta was really funny as she sat Indian style, and on the floor, no less! And my dear Sister Paul, who was looking right back at me! Probably knew every thought that filled this wondering mind. I shyly took a peek in her direction. I couldn't believe it! She smiled and winked at me! Did I really see her do that?

The week-end flew by. I was almost sorry to see it coming to an end. The Sisters played a game of croquet on the lawn while I lazily stretched out in a chair reading a book. I couldn't tell you the name of the book or what it was about. I spent more time peering over the top of the book spying on the Sisters and enjoying their uncharacteristic gaiety. It was such fun to see them joking and laughing together. Sister Marie even accused Sister Florence of cheating during the game! They were all totally human in every respect!

The children would be returning from their home visits this evening. It was very evident that the sisters were back to their normal routines. I felt a sick knot churning in the pit of my stomach as I sat waiting for the first group of children to announce their arrival.

Sometimes watching my friends return to the home was worse than watching them leave. It was hard to see them clinging to their parents begging to stay with them. There wasn't a dry eye in the home on these Sunday evenings when the children returned. I 'll never forget the tear filled eyes and the haunting cries of some of my dearest friends during the night. I would go to their bed and hold onto them tight. I would cry with them and tell them that in the morning they would feel better again. I would whisper rays of hope that they would probably be able to go home permanently very soon. Sometimes that did happen.

There was one girl in particular that I will never be able to get out of my mind. She returned from her visitations with marks on her arms and legs. I wished and prayed that she wouldn't be permitted to ever visit with her father again. No matter how many times her father tried to get help it always ended up with his daughter being hurt. It would take weeks of kindness, love, and patience on the Sisters part to get her to start talking and believing in goodness again. She was one girl that came back from visits dry-eyed and silent. It hurt to see such pain from her broken heart.

I said a silent prayer of thanks knowing I wouldn't have to say good-bye to anyone. I don't think I would look forward to visiting family and relatives knowing that I'd have to say good-bye. Is the hurt that was caused during that short time worth the love of a week end? I just didn't understand.

As the weeks passed and time for weekend visitation arrived, I focused my attention on my special weekend with the sisters and our secret activities. I smiled knowing that I finally didn't mind the weekend visitations and my friends saying good-bye as they greeted their loved ones for a special time. I was looking forward to my own special time alone getting to know more about my loving Sisters.

THE SPORT OF INTERACTION

For as long as I could remember, the boys in the home always had a competitive basketball team. They played games against other teams from nearby schools and during the early winter months they were involved in a basketball tournament. There were kids not only from the neighboring schools but from schools all around St. Louis that participated in the tournament. The tournament brought a lot of excitement to the home and provided the children with weeks of busy preparation and intermingling with "the outside folks" as we commonly referred to them.

Both of my brothers were avid basketball players. I was very proud of their accomplishments. My brothers' names appeared on many of the trophies in the home's trophy case and I was noted for pointing information out to anyone who happened to be standing near the gymnasium. I looked up to both of my brothers with a genuine pride and I wanted everyone to know what neat guys they really were. Plus, it didn't hurt me any to be related to two well rounded brothers.

It was unusual for the girls in the home to play basketball. We shot baskets and dabbled around with the sport but never understood the entire game with its rules and regulations.

Late one November morning, our lay-gym teacher entered the gymnasium. We knew something was about to happen because she was smiling as if she were hiding a secret and exploding inside to share it with someone. Finally, without delay, she told us her exciting news. She was going to become a mother. I remember looking immediately at her slim waist and her flat tummy. I tried to visualize her standing there, off—balance, with an extremely large belly. I just couldn't imagine it! We were happy that our teacher was to become a mother but sad for ourselves because it was inevitable that she would be leaving us. She was a terrific person whom we all adored and would miss dearly. She was one of the few contacts we had on a weekly basis that came from the outside world.

It was a matter of months since our gym teacher had left. We gave her a wonderful good-bye party with a cake and the trimmings. Sister Paul made her some baby clothes and Sister Carlotta made the baby some adorable booties.

One day, Sister Anna announced that a new gym teacher was found and she would start her routine with us the following week. I was never so grateful. It was next to impossible putting up with Sister Anna as a gym teacher. She was ok as nun but as a gym teacher...I was very happy to see her quit. She made us exercise and exercise then play tag at least every other day. When it came to games for gym class, Sister was sorely lacking in the imagination department.

I personally was getting tired of Sister telling us girls to pull our pant legs down on our gym uniforms. We all had a habit of pulling our elastic pant legs way up above our knees. It was just a lot cooler and easier to move around during gym activities. But, in the 1950's, proper ladies didn't expose their legs in such a manner. What if the boys saw us or, Lord help us, what if a benefactor happened to be visiting us on the day we ran around like that?

Our new gym teacher entered the gym with a slam of the door. We were standing around anticipating her entrance. We were hoping she would be as cute and sweet as our last gym teacher. Boy, were we in for a real surprise. "Good golly," I said without thinking. She had a very manly appearance, even though we knew she had to be a woman. Women had to coach girls just as men had to coach boys. Needless to say, disappointment showed on all of our faces.

I thought Sister Anna was bad as a gym teacher. Especially when it came to exercises. Well, she would be considered easy compared to our new teacher. I stretched muscles that I didn't even know I had. Then one day she hit us with the impossible.

"Girls," she said, "we are going to have a competitive basketball team. You will all need a good deal of shaping-up and training but we will compete in a few months and we will win." I wanted to shout, "that's what you think, lady," but I thought I better not. 20 laps around the gym would be more than I could handle in these classes. I had the pleasure of 15 laps around the gym a week ago. Teacher caught me making fun of her behind her back. I never could understand how teachers can see behind their backs. I know one of the girls didn't tell teacher what I was doing. They were all biting on their tongues trying hard not to laugh at me as I acted the fool imitating in a manly sort of way.

Well, the first month dragged on and we practiced and practiced. Basketball was a word that I wished I'd never heard before. I was just too short to shoot baskets and I didn't have the stamina to run back and forth the length of the gym floor for as many times as that game required. You might say that I didn't like anything about basketball. Who knew there were so many rules to any game? Double dribble, charging, jump ball, foul line, etc. This all drove me crazy. I was always getting the whistle blown on me and threatened by teacher that I would have to do extra laps at the end of gym if I violated any more rules. "How dumb," I mumbled under my breath, making sure that Ms. Gym Teacher was on the opposite side of the gym when I made my complaint. I was getting smarter when it came to getting away with insults and my gym teacher.

As the weeks grew into months our basketball team developed. We passed dribbled, pivoted, shot, etc, and. all with the best of them. We didn't have anyone to compare ourselves to except for the boys. I think we were starting to look comparable.

One morning, our gym teacher made her usual entrance as she slammed the door, getting our undivided attention. She had some news to share with us. She knew we would be pleased with the news and just as happy as she was. We were going to have an exhibition basketball game with the St. Joseph's girls. The other boys and girls in the home, along with the sisters, would be present at the game. She further announced that the teachers from St. Joseph's school would be in attendance. I looked at the gym teacher with my mouth wide open as she further stated that St. Joseph's school was a school for deaf girls.

Well, now I'd heard it all. We were going to play a basketball game in front of everyone in the home, including my brothers, visiting teachers and against some girls who couldn't hear a thing going on.

"How can they hear the whistle when they foul"? I shouted, trying to understand what was going on. "They can hear the whistle, miss smarty pants. They do have hearing aides in their ears, you know." "Oh," I replied as I took my seat. I guess that makes sense. They are normal girls like us just a little hard of hearing. I've never seen anyone who was deaf before. This should be a real experience.

The day of the big game finally came. Our teacher told us we were ready and so it must be. We were as ready as we would ever be. We entered the gym with a slam of the door, ready to do battle. The St. Joe girls were already on the basketball court performing warm up laps. The kids and Sisters all clapped for us as we made our grand entrance. Suddenly I was filled with excitement.

I wanted to look good for my brothers and for the Sisters. "We'll cream these girls," I found myself saying out loud. I really thought we were that good.

As the game started I felt a little self conscious as I looked around. These girls appeared taller than we were and had a hungry gleam in there eyes. I tried to smile at one of the girls and she greeted me back with a grind of her teeth. I turned toward another girl and yelled, "Hi, I'm Ruthi." She didn't answer. She nodded her head. Bethy laughed nervously and said, "She didn't hear you, silly, she probably didn't have her hearing aid turned on." Well, I didn't know they could turn their hearing aids on and off. This was something I was going to have to investigate.

As soon as the jump ball proclaimed the start of the game, I was in full action. I captured the ball and dribbled down the court with the full intention of making the first score. One of the St. Joe's girls was on me like the heat of the day. She bounced the ball out of my hand, passed it to another girl on her team and down they ran to the other end of the gym. It was just the first few minutes of the game and already they scored. I had the feeling this was going to be a long game. I only hoped they wouldn't make us look too much like amateurs.

As the second half of the game started, I found myself trying to jump up with my opponent. We were both trying to get a rebound. The ball rolled around the basket rim and seemed to hang suspended in the air for several minutes. As my opponent came down from her jump I felt her elbow crash down on my head causing me to see a million stars. I staggered but refused to go down. I didn't realize it, but after she hit me my mouth blurted out something like you,"big dumb deaf jerk." My head really hurt. I could hear the referee yelling something as her whistle blew.

The girl took one long look at me and mumbled that she was tired of my mouth. She came running at me. I lay on the floor with the girl on top of me. She was pulling my hair and screaming "take it back, you little orphan." After several tries the referee and my gym teacher separated us.

My gym teacher told me to get my wits about me and go to the dressing room. At the same time the referee announced that I was kicked out of the game. I felt very upset and still in a daze but I noticed that the girl from St. Joe's was on her way to the dressing room also.

The game had come to an end. We lost by a mere 10 points. Not too bad for starters. I was too ashamed to come out of the locker room at the end of the game but my gym teacher summoned all of us girls, including me, back to the gym. I had to face the entire home and the girls of St. Joe's. I didn't want to see anyone. I really didn't mean to cause such a ruckus.

As I headed to the stairway, I looked up and saw my opponent walking to the stairway too. I guess she was called back to the gym, too. I looked at the girl and smiled shyly. I wasn't mad at the girl, even though my head and body hurt like the dickens. I didn't mean to hurt her with my words. Even though, she hurt me, too, with her words. Calling me an orphan was just not right. I looked up and was surprised and relieved as she returned my smile. She said, "I'm sorry. I didn't mean to hurt you. " That's when I saw the girl in a different way. She was very pretty and very nice. She talked a little funny but I guess that's the way you talk when you have hearing problems. We shook hands and I let her climb the stairs ahead of me. As she got to the top of the stairs she backed up and pretended to kick at me. She started laughing as I grabbed at her foot, all in a playful mood.

As we entered the gym we were arm in arm laughing. I had made a new friend. Her name was Stella. I hoped we would play basketball together again. I also wished I could play on Stella's team. She was quite good. As we came near the benches where our coaches were sitting we said a cheerful good-bye and Stella did something I had never seen before. She held her hand up and started signing with her fingers. My teacher stood by my side and explained to me that Stella was speaking to me the way that deaf people communicate. She told me that Stella was saying "Until next time my new friend." I hugged myself not knowing what to do and said, "Until next time my friend." We smiled and went our own ways.

I was amazed that the gym was half empty. I was also amazed that my gym teacher expressed, "Good game," to all of us. She smiled at me and tousled my hair as she said, "next time, jump higher, Ruthi." That was it. I wasn't in trouble or anything. I started looking at my new gym teacher in a different way. She really was quite nice. She was also proud of each and every one of us.

As we were heading out the gymnasium door, our gym teacher told us that we would be playing St. Joe's girls again real soon. "This was a very good experience, girls, she said," I think all of us learned a lot today." I was so happy. I would look forward to seeing my new friend, Stella, again. Somehow, this game of basketball wasn't so bad after all. As I passed the trophy case I couldn't help thinking that someday, I'd have my name on a trophy in that trophy case. It will be as big as my brother's and they will be proud of me—providing I don't get kicked out of any more games. A smile crossed my lips as the image of Stella and I rolling around on the gym floor suddenly appeared. What a sight we must have been.

A STOLEN KISS

I was taking the trash can to the ash pit. The ash pit was located behind the garage and the laundry facility, directly on the back side of the home. I waited in anticipation at the ash pit to meet my boyfriend, Donald James. Donald was an amazing boy with dark hair that parted in several directions, making him look like he had just walked out of a wind tunnel. His skin had a dark glow to it. Some say he looked like he needed a good cleaning but I said he looked tan all year long. None of that mattered to me because Donald was to me a Huck Finn look alike. The most interesting characteristic about Donald was his left ring finger. Half of the finger was cut off and never replaced. I can't remember what happened to Donald's finger but it was kind of mysterious to see this lean, gangling boy with messy hair and half a finger. He definitely kept one wondering.

During math class, early in the morning, Donald passed a note to me. He stated in the note that he would like to see me alone. So, knowing I was on trash duty this week, Donald requested that I meet him. He said he would be there and to wait for him, no matter what.

I looked around for Donald but didn't see him. It was starting to get pretty dark outside. While looking in the direction of the orchard I could see the change in the trees as the bark seemed to turn completely black. I cast my glance toward the ball field and I started getting a squeamish feeling down deep in the pit of my stomach. The wind was blowing through the trees and I could hear a rumbling noise. The few leaves that had fallen were whipping around in a circle and in the distance I could hear an owl crying out "Who, who?" Well, I could tell you who, who. It is me, who is going to start running like the dickens in just two seconds if Donald didn't make his presence known and real soon.

I waited a few more minutes when suddenly I heard an unusual sound. It sounded like running footsteps and then the fence rattling. Well, all I could say was, "come on feet—I'm out of here." I started to run to the side of the garage as fast as my legs would carry me. Suddenly, out of nowhere my arms were pinned to my sides as my chest came into contact with a very hard object. The trash can I was carrying was thrown to the ground.

Donald's face loomed in front of my face and he planted a wet, hard—pressed kiss that completely engulfed my lips. I was so astounded that I pushed myself as hard as I could from Donald's grasp, picked up my trash can and hit him as hard as I could right across the top of his head.

Donald yelled and screamed and I could tell I really hurt him. "I'm sorry," I said, "but you shouldn't have scared me like that." Donald replied that all he wanted to do was to give me a kiss. A kiss surely would proclaim to the other boys that I was finally Donald's girl.

I liked Donald very much and I did dream of being kissed someday but I wasn't ready for this! I didn't even enjoy that kiss, much less; he scared me out of my wits. I looked at Donald's face and could see a trickle of blood running from his head. I tried to ease the situation by showing concern and asking if his head hurt badly. "Sure, it hurts like hell!" he said. "You didn't have to hit me so hard like that. And just what am I going to tell Sister when I get back to the dorm?"

I told him to tell Sister that I hit him because he scared me. If I was going to get into trouble it would be worth it since I was feeling so bad about what had happened. Donald didn't reply immediately. He just stood looking at the ground. When he did look at me he asked, in a very quiet voice, if he could give me another kiss the way he had originally planned. I was almost afraid to answer him but gave my permission. I further stated that it had to be a very quick and soft kiss, not like the one he forced on me by the garage.

Donald wiped the blood from his cheek, ran his fingers through his hair and gently cupped my chin with his hand. I stood very still, hoping Donald couldn't hear my rapid heartbeat. I never knew Donald could be so sweet. His kiss was very soft. I almost couldn't feel it. I opened my eyes to see him staring at me with a knowing smile. We had both just entered into a whole new phase of growing up. We would both be looking forward to many more meetings and experimental kissing in the future.

I smiled back at Donald as I picked up my trash can and headed toward the girls side of the home. I felt as though I was floating on a cloud. I couldn't help touching my lips with my fingers and wondering if every girl that had been kissed felt this way. I hoped that Donald enjoyed the kiss as much as I did. As I lay in bed that evening I realized that I could finally admit having experienced a real kiss and, more importantly, I enjoyed the entire experience.

The next day, as I entered the classroom, I looked around to see if Donald was present and if he had gotten into any trouble. He was sitting at his desk watching me as I walked into the room. Our eyes met and he smiled. I knew that everything was all right. His head had a small bandage on it, the evidence of last night's battle for a stolen kiss. Donald wore the bandage as a medal of courage. I had to smile shyly at him.

It was very hard to concentrate on school matters that day. I found myself daydreaming about Donald and wondered if I would always feel like this. I couldn't help giggling whenever I looked his way. Whenever our eyes met, we would quickly glance away but always with a knowing smile tugging at our lips. Thinking back on the episode, I couldn't believe that I had actually hit him in the head with a trash can. What would happen if any of the Sisters had a clue to what was going on? Well, I know we would actually be skinned alive.

As the days passed, the kissing incident became a small memory locked away in my heart. Donald and I was still boyfriend and girlfriend as far as the other kids knew, but there weren't any more kissing episodes.

It was hard to believe that we had just a few more months of seventh grade ahead of us. During this time Sister Robert became very ill. Sister couldn't teach for several days, so one of the other Sisters was sent to the classroom as a substitute for her.

We were a pretty good bunch of kids, as the saying goes. But we had to be good because we lived here in the home full time so; anything that happened in the class followed you around no matter where you were to go.

During class one day, Donald and a few other boys came up with a brainy idea. They had a plan that they would visit us girls in our dormitory during the evening hours. The sisters would be saying their final vespers at approximately 9:00 p.m. This would give them time to leave their dorm and head our way. All was set.

The classroom was filled with buzzing pertaining to the event. As far as Sister Benefice could tell we were the most silent and secretive kids she had ever had to watch. "They were actually a joy," were her exact words.

As the evening hour approached, Sister Paul started having a suspicion that something was about to happen. She knew her girls were up to something. They were being entirely too good and too quiet. But what was going on?

We all took our baths and were ready for bed 15 minutes ahead of schedule. Our homework had been completed in the classroom that day since Sister Robert was sick and there wasn't a complaint from anyone when it was time to complete chores. We were truly a mystery to sister. I'm sure the back of her neck was just crawling.

At approximately 10:00 p.m., as the grandfather clock chimed, we heard a knock on our dormitory door and then another. We knew it had to be the boys but not one girl in the dorm would stir. Suddenly, another knock and the giggles started. I figured we had to open the door before one of the Sisters heard all the commotion. I opened the door and five boys came running into our room. The boys acted like they were crazy. They started jumping on our beds and dancing around like a pack of fools. Donald came up to me and stated, "Let's show everyone how we kiss." All too suddenly I became aware of this horrible situation.

Here stood five boys in an all girls dorm. We really didn't think they would actually come. In fact, we could have made bets that they wouldn't have the nerve. It was funny to think of them sneaking around in the hallways, making their way to our third floor dorm in the dark. But no one really thought they would succeed, much less even try.

As the laughter became louder, the boys became sillier. Donald kept trying to persuade me to give him a kiss and I started to feel panic. I tried to silence the other kids, but the situation was totally becoming out of hand.

Out of nowhere Sister Paul and Sister Florence came running to our room. As they flicked on the lights the scene that lay before them must have been ghastly. The sight of their faces soon silenced the entire room.

Sister Paul showed her complete disappointment in us girls. She just couldn't believe her eyes. It was next to impossible to meet her gaze without turning away. Sister Florence ran rapidly around the room hitting every boy that she could reach. I could have sworn she was going to have a heart attack. She kept getting redder and redder in the face. I felt sorry for the boys but I felt sorrier for us girls. It's not that anything bad really happened. It was just child's play. It was so very, very, wrong. We were very lucky that the Sisters did show up before a real problem occurred.

After the boys were escorted to their dorms, we were instructed to get into our beds and the matter would be handled appropriately the very next day. Sister Paul turned the lights off and wouldn't give any of us girls a chance to speak our mind. She was upset by this commotion. I didn't think she would ever forgive us. I lay restless most of the night feeling very ashamed and sorry for all that had transpired. I would have given anything to take away the hurt that shown in Sister Paul's eyes. I knew the boys would all be punished severely for their actions and I felt a pang of sorrow for them, too. What a situation we had been involved in.

As morning approached we dressed quietly for Mass and waited apprehensively for our punishment. Sister Paul never said a word to any of us girls. We walked quietly to Mass and then afterward to breakfast. We completed our chores and still we waited. School seemed to creep slowly by but still no recourse was at hand. Finally, after the supper dishes had been cleaned and the tables set for the next day, Sister Paul said she was ready to talk to us girls. She told us of her disappointment and how very ashamed she felt knowing that we had betrayed her trust in us. She explained the sight of the previous night when she opened the dormitory door.

She further commented that she loved us and she understood how we felt. Growing up at this particular age was difficult. She told us that no matter what happened or who was to blame, we would all have to earn her trust again. She whispered that she knew in her heart that we would always remain her good little girls.

The tears were on the brim of my eyes as Sister Paul glanced repeatedly in my direction while speaking to us. How I loved this little nun with the stooped shoulders. How I hated disappointing her. I've known her all my life. I remembered the days when she walked briskly and stood tall. When did she become so frail? I vowed then and there that I would prove to her how good I could be and that she could trust me again. I never wanted her to look at me with disappointment again.

As I listened to sister talk I wondered how she became a nun here in the orphan home. How did she know so much about her girls? I bet my bottom dollar that before she became a nun she was a girl full of the dickens just like us. She must have been a beauty, too, because you could see the spark in her light brown eyes.

I couldn't stop the thoughts that suddenly sprang into my mind. I began to wonder—did Sister ever experience a real first kiss? If so—was it a situation like my first kiss? I'm sure Sister Paul became so knowledgeable through her own past experiences. Maybe we're more like her than she ever imagined. I bet that is why she cares so much for us. With these thoughts passing through my mind, I experienced a renewed spirit as I hoped that one day I would grow into an understanding, loving person, just like my dear Sister Paul. I too, would learn to trust and love.

A SPECIAL GIFT

Snow was falling. Everything looked so beautiful and clean in white. The flakes were lazily coming down and it was simply mesmerizing watching them float softly to the ground. The branches on the bush right next to the window were laden with a mixture of ice and snow. I felt sure we would have three feet of snow before the storm ended.

Saturdays and Sundays were wonderful days. No school, no chores, unless you were on kitchen duty. Time was yours to enjoy, for that moment. Today, Sister Carlotta told us we were going to paint the windows with Christmas scenes. The classroom windows were located on the third floor and were at least six feet high. There were a total of 6 windows—3 lined each side of the room. I can still remember the painted scenes from the previous years. I hoped we could do as good a job this day.

Sister Carlotta gathered all the children and issued paint brushes and paints. She explained that we would be working in pairs. Two children painted the top part of the window while two painted the bottom portion.

My friend Patty and I decided to paint Mary holding her new baby, Jesus. Mary was warmly wrapped in a blue mantel. Her hair softly fell about her shoulders as her eyes focused on at her newly born son. Patty and I painted in silence for hours. We were so proud of our accomplishment. My thoughts were not completely on the painting, though; they were on the special event that was soon to take place the following week.

Sister Florence, one of the teachers, was in charge of the Christmas procession. Every year on Christmas Eve, we would have a beautiful Mass and a procession entering the chapel. Children would be dressed as Angels, Shepherds, The Three Wise Men, Joseph and Mary. The Chapel would be decorated in Christmas finery with garlands, lights and a nativity scene.

It was my utmost dream to be picked as Mary. One of the older girls was always selected for that special part. Every year, it seemed, I was selected to be an angel, but it was my fervent hope that my last year at the orphan home I would be selected to be Mary. For some sentimental reason this was very, very important to me. Sometimes I would sit on the bench remembering the faces and names of the girls that had been Mary in the past, but now, those girls were long gone and becoming a fading memory.

The day for selecting the Christmas cast was here and Sister Florence had indeed selected me to represent Mary. For the first time I can remember, I had nothing to say. I nodded my head as Sister read my name for the part and I remember feeling such an overwhelming gratitude in my heart. I'm sure that all the Sisters knew how important this honor was to me. It was a very emotional moment.

A short time later the realization hit me! I had finally been chosen by all the Sisters to represent the most holy mother! All I could think of was the many years gone by when I was never chosen for anything, especially adoptions or visitations, but none of that mattered now, the Sisters had chosen and I was the recipient.

Sister Paul spent a whole evening altering Mary's blue gown for me. I felt like a bride getting ready for her wedding day. Sister Carlotta instructed me on the proper way to walk, so that I wouldn't trip on the floor length gown. She showed me the tender way to hold the baby Jesus in my arms. The evening was fast approaching for the procession and it was very hard to contain my excitement.

While standing alone in the classroom, after donning Mary's dress and waiting for the procession to begin, an overwhelming rush of memories and emotion consumed me. Different events of my childhood years at the orphanage started rushing around in my head.

I remembered as a small but timid child learning to talk with Sister Zita's help. I could see 25 white iron beds in a dormitory, all lined-up in a perfect row. While closing my eyes I could still smell and feel the clean white linens that lay on each bed. The sheets are folded back in a neat roll exposing a soft heavy blanket. I still remember looking under my bed at night—making sure no boogie man was going to grab me in the middle of the night. I remember hugging Sister Paul one Sunday afternoon after she had sewn my favorite winter jumper and my thoughts turned to painting corn-blue flowers on get-well cards with Sister Florence. Choir practices were always uplifting with Sister Gilbert directing us in song while she played the organ. It sure doesn't take much to envision the kitchen smells that wafted through the hallways as Sister Bernadette was busy preparing the evening meals. Sister Robert was very special to me as her eyes held the merriment of laughter while she scolded me for one silly thing or another. And my very special love was Sister Marie, my guardian angel, who was in charge of all functions in the chapel. How I remember the times she would waken me from a tear filled slumber on parent visitation days. The memories are endless.

My first and only wish was to make all my sisters proud of me. I would surely miss them all when my time to leave the home arrived. I still had six more months until then. Sometimes I wish I could stay and become a nun. They wouldn't permit that, though. I already asked. Sister Marie said that 14 years in the home was just too much. She said I needed to try to live in a family setting and that is why my counselors were looking for a foster home placement. I already knew in my heart that I'd be back someday, as Sister Ruth.

Sister Carlotta approached softly. I was still standing in a dreamy state. It was time for Mary to take her place in the procession. As we paraded down the hall toward the chapel, I smiled as the little angels and shepherds walked proudly in step with the music. Was it just last year that I was one of these little angels? And which of these angels would be chosen to be Mary next year? Oh well, this was my important moment now and I wanted to remember every step of the way.

Sister Carlotta placed the baby Jesus in my arms and held the door open for me as I made my grand entrance into the chapel. The lights were low and the candles lit. The decorations were brilliant in green and red. I could feel that all eyes were on me. The choir began singing Silent Night as my feet glided down the path toward the Nativity scene in the front corner of the chapel. I glanced at Father Slattery as I processed toward the manger. Father Slattery acknowledged me with a slight nod of his head and his usual tender smile.

As I placed the baby Jesus in the manger, I couldn't contain the tears that flowed down my cheeks and onto the beautiful blue gown I was wearing. I will always keep the memory of this special moment locked deep within my heart. I will forever carry the love of my Sisters and the pride of my beautiful home within me wherever I go.

As evening approached and I was alone in my bed, I said a special prayer. I prayed that Jesus was happy with me representing His holy mother. I prayed for all my dear friends in the orphanage and hoped they, too, would find their happiness. I prayed for my Sisters who gave me this most memorable Christmas gift—their unconditional gift of love.

PREPARATIONS FOR PICNIC DAY

It was the month of June. What a terrific month for a picnic. The Orphan Home held their annual picnic at this time of the year for the children, the benefactors, the alumni, and the public which included basically anyone who would like to partake of the festivities. All outsiders were welcome. Newspaper Ads proclaimed the upcoming event and preparations were started.

Weeks before the picnic were spent preparing the home for all the expected visitors. The Sisters took full charge and delegated the chores of cleaning, cooking and decorating. When I say full charge I mean as the list grew, the chores were handed out to all. There would be nothing in the orphanage that didn't get a clean swipe or wipe. Do you remember the white glove test? Well, I really think Mother Matilda invented white gloves.

One vision that always made me bubble with laughter was the scrubbing and waxing of the long corridor halls. It took six children abreast to scrub and remove old wax from the hallway floors. Of course there was a big machine that helped do the scrubbing and waxing and Sister Ermgraud was the supreme handler for that job. She would roll up her big sleeves and pin her apron to her bodice. Her skirts would be tucked up in her waist band while her black stockings and black pumps were in clear view, adding to her humorous attire.

The six children abreast would be on hands and knees trying to keep ahead of the "electric driven monster," with sister hanging on at the helm.

One of the children would sit on top of the motor during buffing time. This added a little extra weight to the big machine. This process afforded the floors an extra shine with a tint of celestial glow.

Sister Paul was in charge of sewing and mending the red, white and blue banners that would be hung in splendid array. A German band, always an important part of the picnic, included musicians dressed in the traditional German attire. The "um-pa-pa" could be heard echoing through the courtyards and hallways as an added rendition of "Roll out the Barrel" claimed the favorite tune.

Sister Florence and Sister Gilbert prepared the chickens for frying while numerous girls spent the afternoons shredding cabbage for coleslaw. Apple sauce and apple butter were carried up carefully from the cellar and hundreds of potatoes, eyes and all, stared at us for peeling.

Sister Zita, with impeccable sight, made sure the dishes and silverware were spotless. She was a master at setting a beautiful table. It didn't matter the occasion, she loved the challenge.

Many alumni came back to the orphan home during this special time. They would set up game booths and prepare crafts to fill the booths. They helped Sister in the kitchen as instructions were clearly dictated to deep fry the chicken. Benefactors and patrons spent time sampling the beer while setting up the beer stand—to us children that stand seemed to be the most popular stand of the entire event.

There were car rides and pony rides for the small children and an enormous Ferris wheel which brought screams of excitement at the mere sight of it. The Ferris wheel wasn't the only wheel turning as the girls huddled together betting on which boy would ask them to take a ride on the gigantic ride.

The picnic day usually started with a 12:00 noon mass. People from all around attended the service. The small chapel was packed full. Voices blended together in unison as our beloved Sister Gilbert played the piped organ. She was always in the proper key and demanded punctual songs.

Father Slattery looked animated as his white vestments flowed with his every movement. This added a touch of heavenly splendor to the scene. As the service came to an end all eyes were focused on Father, waiting in anticipation for him to dismiss the crowd so the picnic festivities could begin.

If I close my eyes today and listen intently I can still envision the activities that transpired during the home's picnic day. It took dedication and hard work by everyone involved to make this event a success. We became a family preparing for a big celebration while partaking of great food, toe-tapping music and all the laughter that the word "picnic" could hold.

The children learned a lot during that special time. We learned that hard work and togetherness could make anything possible. We learned the pride of keeping a clean and spotless home. We learned to appreciate the Sisters and how to be prepared and improvise no matter what the situation.

A QUICK LAST YEAR

While wandering down the driveway, in a dreamy sort of way, I couldn't help saying a thankful prayer for this beautiful Saturday in the month of May. The sky was bright blue and the warmth of the sun wrapped the earth in a nurturing spring blanket. This certainly was one of those lazy, relaxing kinds of days that one would dream of on a cold winter night.

Moments ago, a cleansing spring rain had just come to an abrupt stop. The rain was sorely needed after the year's drought. The entire yard was a muddy mess from the mixture of snow and early spring rain. Life was dismal then, but now, the sun was breathing new life back into the earth.

As I walked down the path, I breathed in the heady smell of bright pink roses that lined the driveway. I can still close my eyes and remember that beautiful scent. The Sisters prided themselves on growing those very special roses.

Off to the side of the driveway was a path that led to the grotto. I spent quiet moments at the grotto gazing at the statue of Mary. The grotto consisted of gray stones and the flooring had bright green moss running between the gray slates. I truly believe that most of my fervent prayers were said while kneeling at the grotto, surrounded by the sounds and sights of nature and breathing in the fresh outdoor air.

I had just turned 14 years old in January. I felt the stir of womanhood beginning and in love with the world that surrounded me. I watched a plane as it glided through the clear blue sky. The sun casting its glow on the plane's silver wing almost blinded me. Wouldn't it be wonderful to be up in that plane flying to an important place? Somewhere—anywhere? I would love to be flying to Morocco to meet Princess Grace. She truly lived up to her name. "Grace," "Oh to be a lady with such qualities."

I continued walking past the grotto and onto the path that led to the beautifully landscaped grounds of the home. While rounding the corner of the pathway my eyes gazed at an unfamiliar person working in the garden. I heard that we had just acquired a new grounds keeper to help with the heavy work. Old Andy, our head maintenance man, was getting on in years and had suffered a heart attack during the winter months. We all worried about Andy and prayed for his recovery. He never did bounce back all the way. I imagine his age had something to do with his slow healing process. Well, I was sure curious about this handsome strong person working away in the garden. He was only a few feet away and already I could tell—he was something.

His name was Carl. He was a refugee from Hungary and spoke very broken English. It wasn't difficult to communicate with him; he understood a little and smiled a lot. It took me all of one day to find out all about him.

I didn't know if it was the spring season—or if it was my age—you know how the hormones are at age fourteen. But I really fell for this handsome, lonely man. I introduced myself to Carl and tried very hard not to stare at him. His smile was just as beautiful as his eyes. I suddenly realized the dilemma this man put me into. How on earth could my heart be beating so wildly over this man when I was suppose to be thinking of my boyfriend Donald James?

As the spring season developed into mid—summer, I used every excuse known in the book to be around Carl. I volunteered for extra duty in the orchard, in the garden, even in the laundry room. My eyes never wandered far from his side. I really became proficient with the excuses that abetted in my ploy.

I found out that Carl was a very lonely man. He didn't have any family here in America. He certainly was working in the right place—an orphan home. He was such an easy person to talk to and to work with. His smile was genuine and so were his manners. I could feel something special happening between us. It wasn't anything foul or dirty and it was more than a mere infatuation. I believe it was a true out and out friendship with a little tinge of love. It certainly brought excitement to my lonely, boring life.

Carl was washing the windows to our dormitory one summer day. He was on one of the super tall ladders. I was just returning from my chores in the laundry room when I saw the ladder leaning on the side of the building. The sight of Carl on the extension ladder made me think of trapeze artists flying through the air at the circus. They were so lean and exciting. My heart started pounding as I rushed up the three flights of stairs to our dormitory. It lifted my spirits when I saw my smiling, handsome friend scrubbing at the window. As I entered the room, Carl smiled and then told me he had a present for me. He had hoped he would run into me before his job was finished. I couldn't imagine what kind of present Carl would have for me but I was truly humbled to think that he cared enough to do such a thing.

Carl disappeared down the ladder, and within a few seconds he came back up and handed me a photograph of himself, dressed in blue jeans and a cowboy shirt. His arms were folded across his chest and he was leaning against a fence post. What a great gift! I was so excited and placed the picture on my side of the dresser. This way I could look up at Carl from my bed. My friend would always be with me. I smiled with sheer joy, for now my side of the dresser wouldn't be bare anymore. Now I, too, had a photograph to display with pride.

Upon seeing the photo on the dresser, Sister Paul was mortified. She questioned me about my feelings and friendship with Carl but she never put me down or claimed that anything was wrong. How clever and sweet of her. Looking back on it now, I admire her for understanding her girls the way she did.

As the summer turned into fall Carl informed me that he had another surprise for me. He was building a model ship and had just completed it. He named the ship <u>Ruthi</u> , after me. He painted my name in gold letters on the back of the ship for all to see. Carl was so proud of his accomplishment that he wanted to share his talent with some of the Sisters.

He took the boat up to the main office for Sister Minulphia and Sister Anna to view. I was so excited for the sisters to see his beautiful boat that I ran like the dickens to view his presentation from the opposite doorway. I could have won a gold medal in the 100 yard dash as I ran up the double flights of stairs two at a time. I just knew the sisters would appreciate Carl's hard work. I perched myself in the doorway so I had a clear view of what was going on and I listened intently to what transpired.

I was shaken to the core when the two sisters started questioning Carl about his relationship with me. They asked him, why would he name a boat after me? Sister Anna said that she didn't like the idea that I displayed a photograph of Carl on my dresser. The sisters didn't even say that they liked Carl's boat.

I couldn't hear Carl's reply but I could tell he was very frustrated. Sister Anna slammed the boat on the desk. I almost came unglued as I watched the episode unfurl before me. The boat must have broken in several pieces as sister pounded it on the desk top.

Sister Minulphia proceeded to scold Carl and told him that his actions would cause the termination of his job. He was to leave by the end of the week. I couldn't believe that this was happening. I wanted to yell and scream at Sister. I wanted to tell her how wrong she was but I did nothing but stand in the doorway in silent denial.

As life came back into my legs I ran fast as I could, down the stairs and out the door. I had to reach Carl and let him know how sorry I was. I couldn't believe that he lost his job all because of me. I couldn't believe that the sisters spoke so crudely and had broken his beautiful boat that he was so proud of. I couldn't even imagine the hours and time it took to complete his project.

I tried to yell out to him as he quickly rounded the path leading to his living quarters. I thought he didn't hear me, so I yelled again. "Carl," I yelled, "I'm so sorry for everything." He turned sharply and stared into my anxious eyes.

"I loved it here," he said quietly, "and you my little Ruthi will be graduating in just a few short months. I must say goodbye for now, but I will be back to see you on graduation day, my little friend. You can count on Carl."

I never spoke about Carl to anyone after that day. He left during the dark evening hours.

I kept his promise to return locked away in my heart. I couldn't wait until graduation day; I was excited just thinking about seeing him again. The months ahead passed by slowly. I had so many mixed emotions about graduation day. I couldn't tell anyone about Carl's plan and in a way I didn't want to believe that there would be a chance he might not make it.

My thoughts about leaving the home soon closed in on me. How could I leave the Sisters and the other children? This was my life, my home. I didn't want to enter "the outside" world as we called it. There was so very much to think about.

Suddenly, a decision was at hand. I would become one of the nuns. I would become Sister Ruthi and live here forever in my home. On the other hand, if I did take the vows and become a nun I could never marry and someday have my own special family. It hurt to think of so many possibilities.

Graduation was just days away. There were six of us girls and five boys graduating the second Sunday in June. Sister Paul announced that we would all receive brand new graduation outfits. We never had brand new clothes before, so this was adding to my excitement. All the clothes we wore throughout these years were hand-me-downs. The sisters sewed and patched and cleaned and altered. I still have to laugh when I think back at the different outfits that were passed down to me.

I started reflecting back to another time when I was younger. One of the older girls named Mary Ann had become the apple of my brother's eye. Among the outfits she wore was a beautiful multi-color flower dress. I knew without a doubt that some day that dress would be mine. I never knew what happened to that dress. It was probably in the rag bin by the time I was able to wear it. But looking back, I sure thought that dress was something exquisite.

When graduation day arrived I stood alone in the dormitory. I gazed into the long mirror located on the opposite wall and saw a person that I would never have guessed to be me. I looked beautiful. I was almost scared by what I saw. Was this truly the little girl with long banana curls that used to ride in the apple wagon? The person looked back at me and I became saddened by what lay ahead for me.

I had so many doubts, so many expectations. I was excited about starting my new life with my foster parents—the word parent sounded foreign to my ears. My eyes appeared happy but there was a sadness grabbing my heart that I couldn't shake. I longed for this day to come but now that it was here, I wished I had just a little more time left with my Sisters in the home. There was so much I needed to say to them.

My thoughts wandered to Carl. Would I see him at the graduation celebration? Lately, he didn't occupy my thoughts or dreams. I just wished him well and hoped that he was happy with a new job. I hoped he started building a new model ship and I also hoped he would name it after me.

There were so many faces that spanned my time at the home. I was thinking and agonizing over my life here much too much. How could I possibly leave? I had to keep telling myself to take one moment at a time and things would work out. I never felt so alone as I did on my graduation day. The thought of leaving and going to a foster home nagged me the entire day.

The graduation ceremony began with a special Mass. Father Slattery was still so tall and handsome even with his hair tinted with a little gray. Goose bumps pimpled my flesh as his deep voice rang out from the altar. I'd never hear that strong voice again. I tried to change my train of thought as I looked at Sister Marie, my guardian angel. She must have spent hours fussing over the beautiful roses that decorated the chapel. The choir and Sister Gilbert would have one less voice to raise in celestial harmony without me and tomorrow, well, that would be the last time that I would look upon the reddened face of dear Sister Bernadette.

I had to remind myself again before exploding with a million tears that tomorrow was another day and today was for celebrating. Most of my classmates would leave with their parents or relatives today, so I needed to put aside my thoughts and be with my orphanage family for one last time.

It didn't really surprise me that Carl never made it to graduation. I was a little disappointed but not surprised. I couldn't resist the urge to walk around the home's grounds one more time. I was trying to leave an everlasting impression in my mind of all that I held dear. The softball games, the wagon rides, baking apples, picking roses, praying at the grotto and saying the Stations of the Cross. My first kiss behind the ash pit and the cold winter days spent sleigh riding in the orchard laughing with my dear Sisters.

It was truly the hardest thing I ever had to endure when I said good bye to my friends the evening of graduation. One by one I watched them leave and prayed silently that they would find the happiness and peace that they so deserved. My heart cried out with love with each good-bye hug. This would be my last night with my Sisters in my home.

Alone, I stood in the entrance way the next day. I readied myself to make my exit with the help of my caseworker. I quietly put my suitcase on the floor and made my way across the hallway into the chapel. This was always my own special place that I referred to as the "heart of the home." I gazed upon the statues of Mary and then Joseph. So many times I talked over all my worldly problems with these statues. I took a final look at the altar where I made my first Holy Communion and held the tiny infant Jesus during the Christmas procession. I will always see the

Sisters working around the chapel, placing new linens on the altar. I will always hear the pipe organ and see Sister Gilbert directing the choir.

My eyes gazed upon the highest window of the home and my thoughts were filled with my very special friend, Tina. It's funny, I thought, for she would always be here at the home peering out from that window. She was the only one of us that would not be leaving, for she had found her permanent dwelling. I sat for a few more moments then turned to make my exit. Somehow, I got the courage to do what I knew had to do. I walked quietly out the chapel doors, picked up my suitcase and walked down the long flight of stairs on shaky knees. The grandfather clock in the hall chimed the hour and I looked upon the picture of the guardian angel protecting the two small children as they walked down the pathway. I said a simple but quick prayer that the guardian angel would protect me this day and help me walk down my lonely path. I will always make the Sisters proud of me, I vowed. They gave us strength and taught us to look forward to each new situation. Look your fears squarely in the eye and hold your head up high and never, never, look back...only forward.

I stepped into my caseworker's car. Turning, I wanted to have one final look at my beloved home. I felt so very lucky and extremely proud to have called St. Vincent's my home. I didn't have a clue to what the future had in store for me. I could only hope that my past would continue to give me courage so I could succeed with each step of my new beginning. "I'll make you proud, I whispered," as my nose pressed tightly against the car's window. I will always love my very special place. For it was truly my home and it will always remain so. But oh how I will miss my dear Sisters!

As the car glided through the protective gates, my thoughts conjured up a picture. Sister Paul was scolding a little girl with long blonde hair. Their eyes met and a tender smile played across Sisters lips as she hugged the child tightly to her breast. "Good-bye," I whispered, I will always love you."

EPILOGUE

This book of short stories took quite a few years to conclude. I've always dabbled with writing but poetry was what I relied on to convey mood swings, remembrances and gifts that I created from the heart.

One fall day while feeling in a quiet mood my thoughts started running rampant with visions of the past. The thoughts of the orphanage filled my waking hours and before long I had an overwhelming urge to pay a visit to my childhood home and open up the memories that I had suppressed for so many years.

As I looked back at my years in the orphanage I recalled the childhood adventures that I had innocently experienced. I could see the humor, love, endurance and extreme patience that the Sisters showed daily as they attended to their chores. They performed so effortlessly their many tasks, with a stamina that had to have been brought on by a much higher power than most of us have yet to understand.

I tried to compare the raising of so many children in the present day to that of yesterday but the task seemed utterly impossible. Each child that I witnessed in the home had extreme emotional needs brought on by this world as we currently know it. I found that nothing could compare to the yesterdays I knew. It must be that God grants special qualities only to those who love and serve without question.

While walking through the corridors and dormitories I relived the times and days spent in this very special place. As I walked around the grounds I was astounded at how much smaller they appeared to my grown-up eyes. My excitement mounted as I grasped my hands together while climbing the stairs to the chapel, "The heart of the home," as I always refer to it. It was still just as beautiful as my memories preserved it. I felt an instant power of peace surround my being as the sun filtering through the stained glass windows painted the pews in colors of splendor.

I was truly inspired by my visit and realized how much I missed these feelings of past comfort. I felt indebted to the benefactors and to the dear Sisters as my gaze rested upon a newly installed plaque that was dedicated to the entire order of Sisters who served the children of the home.

The home, that used to be run by the Sisters, is now run by a highly competent staff of lay people. Their leader and director is one of the most dedicated and sincere people that I have had the privilege to know. He listens with intent and wears his emotions with a strong but tender attitude. The kind of child that resides in the home is very special and ridden with emotions that need nurturing and explanation. I thought seeing the Sisters replaced with lay administrators would go against my belief in the purpose of serving these children. How wrong I was. The same grit and love is displayed daily to the children just as it was some 150 years ago.

As the children leave the home to become productive citizens in the world, they take with them a form of independence from the things that they have learned through suffering and heartache. There seems no escaping suffering and pain, mental or physical—it is a part of living and learning. The ache of loneliness and disillusionment caused by hurt can only make one stronger. The disappointments in life don't have to destroy us they can become our teacher. If we become aware of our limitations we can then gain courage and determination. We can become strong and independent.

The END of my story is really a whole new beginning—for how could one end something that has no ending? My history, no matter how many roads it has taken, is still in the making. This too will be the future of each child as they step through the threshold of St. Vincent's doors on their way to their new beginning. I wish them happiness and more importantly I wish them a wealth of wonderful memories.

HISTORY TIDBITS

The St. Vincent's Home celebrated its Sesquicentennial commemoration in June of 2000. It seems an impossible realization those 152 years of service has been provided for thousands upon thousands of children that have walked through St. Vincent's doors. I find the history of the home very interesting when comparing it to the history of our country and of St. Louis. Here is a little piece of history in the making that I think you will enjoy.

1840—In these early years millions of immigrants came to the United States. Many settled in the city of St. Louis. During that decade, the city nearly quadrupled in size, reaching a population of 77,000 of which 23,000 were new German immigrants.

1849—The city of St. Louis suffered two major disasters. A horrible fire that started on a steamboat burned for two days. The fire spread to 23 boats and the sparks soon made there way to 430 buildings in a 15-block area. Many people died and many became homeless. Meanwhile, St. Louis was in the midst of a cholera epidemic which spread by arriving immigrants. As summer progressed, deaths rose to as many as 1,000 people per week. Needless to say that at the end of both tragedies many children were left orphaned and the homeless was numerous.

June of 1850—priests and laymen made an appeal to the German Catholics of the city to consider pooling their limited resources to build a German Orphan Home so that support and education might be provided for the helpless orphans. The appeal found an immediate response and the orphan home was in the making. A plot of ground was bought on Hogan street for the sum of $ 950.00.

July 3, 1851—Five sisters of St. Joseph of Carondelet took charge of the new home and children. The sisters handled the day-to-day operation of the home as well as the education of the children in the German Language. The First orphan child, Anna Schwerdt arrived at the home on July 25, 1851.

1854—The orphanage experienced its first calamity. It was the dread Cholera epidemic that led to the foundation of the Home. Within a brief two weeks, one sister and fourteen children fell victim to cholera. In the year prior to the cholera outbreak, there were 40 boys and 30 girls in the home. This was the same year that Kansas-Nebraska Act Repealed the Missouri Compromise. This repeal perpetuated slavery. In 1854 there were nearly ninety-thousand slaves in the state of Missouri.

1867—The First Women's Suffrage Association In Missouri.

1872—Small pox epidemic invaded St. Louis and the children of the home. All through the summer months smallpox cases occurred, one child died due to this disease.

June 13, 1875—The home celebrated its Silver Jubilee. Three former students who became priests stood at the altar in the Chapel to offer praise and thanksgiving.

One of the students, John Schweltter, a fun-loving student remembered: About 16 boys used to wash and we all wore wooden shoes while we did the washing. When we went from the wash house to the dining room for lunch, we used to run around the table in the dining room, which had a wooden floor. You might imagine what noise this made. We did this until Sister Superior came to stop us. To us, it was a lot of fun, but not for the sisters.

1887—Electric Streetcars were introduced to the St. Louis area.

1888—A celebration of thanks was written in the St. Louis newspapers. The Sisters of St. Joseph who conducted the Orphan Home for nearly 40 years will transfer their administration to another community. The Sisters of Christian Charity came to assume the duties of the orphanage. They found 141 children placed in their care and an increasing number in the future.

1889—Spanish American War Begins.

June 24, 1900—The Golden Jubilee of the Orphan Home was celebrated.. 198 children lived at the home. The home has cared for nearly 2,000 children in this 50 year span.

1904—The Worlds Fair held in Forest Park, St. Louis, Missouri. The Louisiana Purchase Exposition in St. Louis showcased the Midwest's and the nation's human and technological advancements. It attracted thousands of visitors from around the world. The home was now in its 54th year.

1910—A 20 acre plot in Normandy Park was purchased for $18,000. This site would soon hold the new orphan home as we know it today.

1915—Pageant and Masquerade celebrating 150 the anniversary of St. Louis.

June 25, 1916—the cornerstone for the New St. Vincent Orphan Home was set.

August 8, 1917—The children move into their new home in Normandy.

The United States joins WW1 in progress.. The United States declares War on Germany. The United States suffers over 350,000 casualties during its relatively brief involvement in WW1.

War in Europe fuels anti-German passions in Missouri. Strong feelings about Germany and the culture had developed mobs of menacing citizens, whipped into frenzy by war fever, and intimidated their fellow citizens into ending decades of German language education.

A papal delegate addressed the crowd and the anti-German sentiment by saying. "You have built this orphanage to help the poor and abandoned children of your nationality and faith...You have done a great service to the Church and to the State. If they ask for more evidence of your patriotism, point to this building!"

March 1919—After WW1 influenza strikes the home. More than one hundred children were afflicted. Two sisters and four children died from the sickness.

1922—The home on Hogan Street was finally sold to Father Timothy Dempsey. This became home to many working men and women.

1924—A Grotto was built on the homes grounds as a memorial to the seventy-fifth anniversary of the foundation of the order of the Sisters of Christian Charity and the commemoration of the fiftieth anniversary of the sisters' arrival in the United States. The Grotto was modeled after the famed shrine of Lourdes, France.

1925—The Diamond Jubilee of the home was celebrated. In the 75 years of service, more than 3300 boys and girls have called St. Vincent's their home.

1927—Charles Lindbergh and the Spirit of St. Louis take solo flight across the Atlantic.

1929-32—The Great Depression was in force after the stock market crash of 1929. Americans experienced suffering like never before. Farm income shrank by 50% and Industry was performing at half capacity. 32,000 businesses failed as did 1500 banks, wiping out the life savings of millions of Americans. On-quarter of the work force was out of work and charities could not keep up with the demand for assistance.

1930—St. Joseph's shrine was dedicated to the home. This was part of the Home's 80th Anniversary.

1935—Social Security Act Passed. This program was developed to provide services to individuals in the event of retirement, sickness, disability, death and unemployment. The program also included aid to dependent children and child welfare. This new program provided some relief to families who typically turned to organizations like St. Vincent's for help.

1939—Two former students of the home were united in marriage in the chapel of the home.

1940—The first Boy Scout troop was organized at the home.

December 7, 1941—Two Alumni of the home lost their lives in the raid on Pearl Harbor. December 8 the United States officially joins WW11 at the close of the war in 1945, it is estimated that over 415,000 military personnel had given their lives in the war.

June 3, 1950—The children of the home presented a pageant entitled: Of Such is the Kingdom, at the Opera House of Kiel Auditorium, in downtown St. Louis. This was the Centennial Celebration of the home.

June 27, 1950—United Nations sends troops to Korea.

1959—St. Vincent's underwent a major remodeling project. The home was updated and the children's living arrangements changed from a congregate system to a new group system with apartments.

1961—The Home opened its doors to the children from Cuba. At this time, many Cubans sent their children to the United States rather than have them indoctrinated in Communism. The home was one of many homes that offered its facilities to help elevate the burden that the Miami Diocese was feeling. In taking in these children St. Vincent's had played a small part in the struggle between Catholicism and Communism.

November 22, 1963—A nation grieves the death of John F. Kennedy.

March 8, 1965—The First U. S. Troops land in Vietnam.

1965—The Jefferson Expansion Memorial was completed in downtown St. Louis.

1968—Dr. Martin Luther King, Jr. was assassinated and riots broke out across the United States.

1975—St. Vincent's celebrates its 125th anniversary.

Early in 1987—St. Vincent Home for children was faced with the realization that the population of the home was changing. In the 138 years of the homes history the children now come from a changed population. The children, more damaged, more alienated and consequently needier, than the orphan conceived in love, remembering happier days or the child of a broken home who still has the love of one or both parents. The Home no longer called orphanage is now a special facilities place we call Residential Treatment Center. In order to better meet the needs of these children, a program was initiated to re-educate and reorganize the staff members of the home. This staff is highly trained to understand and cope with the children of special needs.

1988—The Sisters of Christian Charity celebrate 100 years of service to St. Vincent's home.

January 16, 1991—Begins U.S. involvement in the Persian Gulf War.

September 1992—The school opens with a complete lay teaching staff. This was the first time in the history of the home that no teachers would be called, "Sister."

1993—The Great Flood. Many people were affected by this flood here in St. Louis.

1996—The last two sisters leave the home.

June 2000—St. Vincent's celebrates it's Sesquicentennial. 150 years of dedication and service. The years continue on and so does the home's commitment.

For 152 years St. Vincent's has been committed to providing a loving environment for children in need. Yesterday, it provided for the children who were orphaned and/or who were products of a broken home. Today, it serves the children of a different need that live in the home which is now called St. Vincent's Residential Treatment Center. These children too, are very special and in need of our love, support and understanding.

AUTOBIOGRAPHY

As a child it was through my ardent imagination that writing became my saving trait. For 14 years of my life I called St.Vincent's Orphanage, my home. I have two older brothers that grew up in the home with me but we never had the union that children normally have while growing up in a "regular family" setting. We shared many experiences together, all of which strengthened our character, allowing us to conquer any new challenges that came our way.

I have always loved to read poetry and eventually I put pen to paper and began to write my own poetry and short stories. This became my escape from the real world as I mixed words and feelings together combined from the experiences that I shared in my youth. It didn't matter if the words were funny or sad—it became a source for emotions.

This book of short stories is about the orphan home and my wonderful years growing up there. I consider this as one of my greatest accomplishments and one of those "must do" things.

I left the orphan home in June, 1962. I was placed in a foster home and this is where my "family" experiences began. I lived with a loving foster family for two years and then, at the age of seventeen, I ventured out on my own.

I met my husband Bob, at the age of eighteen and immediately fell in love with him. He was and still is the handsomest man I ever met and my best friend. We have shared 38 wonderful years of marriage and we are still going strong. We were blessed with two daughters, Shelly and Kathleen and one son, Dan. We also enjoy and adore our three grandchildren: Zachary, Chelsea Kaiah and Joe. They keep us active and add so much love to our lives.

Throughout the years I have always found time to write and to read to my children and grandchildren. When my children were in elementary school I ran a summer program for the neighborhood children and became a volley-ball and softball coach. This was a hoot and when we look back on those years—we miss the fun-filled days. I was the volunteer physical education teacher, in my children's' private school. This lasted for five years. My children claimed I was harder on them than I was on the other children in the school. That could have been true, but, they knew I cared and loved them above all else. When my youngest daughter started first grade it was time for me to get a full-time, paying job. I started out working at a public school as a teacher's aide. After a few short years, I became a school secretary. After eighteen years, I was promoted as secretary to the Assistant Superintendent of schools and presently, celebrating my 20th year, I am the Superintendent's secretary. I have always loved children and enjoy working and growing with them.

My favorite books and authors are <u>Little Women</u> by Louisa May Alcott and <u>Pride and Prejudice</u> by Jane Austin. I love romantic novels and a variety of short stories. As a girl, I enjoyed reading the Nancy Drew mysteries. Currently I have subscriptions to the following magazines: <u>HOME</u>, <u>Country Living, Better Homes and Gardens</u> and a variety of other Country decorating magazines.

My other passion in life is arranging dried floral displays. I especially enjoy making seasonal wreaths, country dried floral pieces and creating floral arrangements. Gardening and spending time with my family are also important to me.

My husband and I love being fans of the St. Louis RAMS football team and the Cardinal baseball team. St. Louis has been very supportive of all sports and a good sports town to raise athletic kids. My son won a college scholarship through soccer. He was a very committed player. So you can understand that sports are very big in our home.

The majority of our married life my husband and I have worked together to build classic hot rod cars. We started with a 1929 Model A Ford and a 1951 Mercury Low Rider. As the years passed we acquired many new friends throughout the country by touring with the family in our beautiful cars. Years later we sold our hot rods to build a front-engine Dragster. It ran on nitro fuel and we raced it at all the local race tracks. My husband's dream was to be in the 200 mile an hour club, and his dream came true at the Indianapolis Speedway! We ran 204 in competition. The Dragster required a lot of work and it was a real money pit. I worried and lived in fear that my son would want to drive the Dragster and was truly relieved when we sold the Dragster and got back to building hot rods. Over the past years, we have completed a 51 Chevy

Sedan and my dream car, a 32 Hi-Boy Roadster. It is really beautiful. We are currently working on a 53 Ford Pick-up truck that will be used as an advertising tool in the next phase of my life.

In February of 2007, I will retire from my career in education. I plan to take on a whole new adventure—opening my own quaint shop which will specialize in seasonal country decor and custom floral decorations. The Sisters of the home have taught me well. I will never have idle hands which they claimed are the devil's workshop.

I look forward to continuing to learn and experience life to its fullest. I have been blessed with so much to share.

769406